SPIRIT DRUMMING

SPIRIT DRUMMING

A GUIDE TO THE HEALING POWER OF RHYTHM

GABRIEL HORN

WHITE DEER OF AUTUMN

STERLING ETHOS

New York

STERLING ETHOS
New York

An Imprint of Sterling Publishing Co., Inc.
1166 Avenue of the Americas
New York, NY 10036

STERLING ETHOS and the distinctive Sterling Ethos logo are registered
trademarks of Sterling Publishing Co., Inc.

ISBN 978-1-4549-2150-9

Distributed in Canada by Sterling Publishing Co., Inc.
c/o Canadian Manda Group, 664 Annette Street
Toronto, Ontario, Canada M6S 2C8
Distributed in the United Kingdom by GMC Distribution Services
Castle Place, 166 High Street, Lewes, East Sussex, England BN7 1XU
Distributed in Australia by NewSouth Books
45 Beach Street, Coogee, NSW 2034, Australia

For information about custom editions, special sales, and premium and corporate
purchases, please contact Sterling Special Sales at 800-805-5489 or
specialsales@sterlingpublishing.com.

Manufactured in China

2 4 6 8 10 9 7 5 3 1

www.sterlingpublishing.com

Design by Lorie Pagnozzi
Decorative elements by iStockphoto.com and Shutterstock.com

CONTENTS

PART ONE

FROM PAST TO PRESENT, THE DRUMMING

The original attitude of the American Indian toward the Eternal, the "Great Mystery" that surrounds and embraces us, was as simple as it was exalted. To him it was the supreme conception, bringing with it the fullest measure of joy and satisfaction possible in this life.

—OHIYESA (DAKOTA) FROM *THE SOUL OF THE INDIAN*

Faster

And the drum sounds

As the spirits move closer . . .

—CHIEF DAN GEORGE (CO-SALISH) FROM *MY HEART SOARS*

Everything I know I learned by listening and watching. Now-a-days people learn out of books instead. Doctors study what man has learned. I pray to understand what man has forgotten.

—VERNON COOPER (LUMBEE) FROM *WISDOMKEEPERS*

CHAPTER ONE

SPIRIT DRUMMING WITHIN THE NARRATIVES

In a universe wide as daylight and bright as starlight, there is the potential for unlimited possibilities and unimaginable diversity. This enables us to think and perceive ourselves and the world and the universe in a much more humble and open way, for the potential within us can only be limited by the way we allow ourselves to think.

When you sit alone in your space of spirit drumming, you reconnect to that which connects you to all things. Some call it Spirit and think of the collective spirit as the Great Spirit, the sum total of all spirit. For me, it is the incomprehensible something I learned to call the Great Holy Mystery. The drum I beat upon and on which I sing my songs; the beat I make with my drumstick, and the songs themselves are all of the Mystery. Some came to me in dreams. Some I learned. Some become spontaneous. I am tapping that part of myself that is Spirit. But the spirit does not belong to me. It is not *my* spirit, it is the spirit of the Great Mystery that exists within me, that exists in all things, and in which all things exist.

Unimaginable. Indefinable.

Whether you choose to sit with your drum alone, or in a circle of others, imagine if each individual brings such awareness to the circle. The experience will be focused, the intent will be strong, and the potential for achieving the communication we are seeking with that deep down part of ourselves that is our own center will be pure. We are here now in this moment on our journeys, wanting to be good people in this world. Perhaps then, with drums in our hands, we can achieve what the late Oglala holy man, Black Elk, describes as the "first real peace."

The first peace, which is the most important, is that which comes within the souls of human beings when they realize their relationship, their oneness, with the universe and all its powers, and when they realize that at the center of the universe dwells *Wakan Tanka*, and that this center is really everywhere, it is within each of us. This is the real peace; all the others are but reflections of this.

—BLACK ELK (LAKOTA)

Imagine . . .

If you choose to be part of this spirit drumming with me now, come with an open mind. And, please, remove your watch. You don't want to insult the power of natural time. Yes, you can peek at your watch on the table if you need to, if you have a meeting to attend, or a job to do, or when you think someone is expecting you, say, a child to be picked up at school. For this is the time to allow the acquired teachings and narratives of *Spirit Drumming* to teach the things that maybe you have forgotten: the simplest of things you did as a child when you picked up a stick and beat it on the ground, or when you clapped your hands, or tapped your foot to the beat of a song, or when you once felt the conscious joy of rhythm and relationship with the Earth and the universe.

If it were me, I wouldn't have my cell phone turned on, either. Remove the technology of distraction; maintain the philosophy of natural interaction.

In the old way, through observation, we learned a good deal about how to do things. Watching not the artificial time on the clocks on walls or strapped on our wrists, but the way the Sun travels across the Sky. The Moon as she waxes and wanes. The solstice and equinox. The birds building their nests: watching . . . how respectful and quiet the adults were around the drum. Watching . . . how children were taught to be respectful and quiet around sacred things and moments as well. Nothing else could be tolerated. Watching . . . a man placing pinches of tobacco on the drum head and offering gratitude. Watching . . . the people using the smoke of sweetgrass and sage to cleanse the drum and drumsticks and even themselves, freeing their minds of feelings and energies not healthy for a ceremony. They listened . . . if someone told the story of a symbol he or she chose to paint on a drum, and through listening, they learned that everything has spirit and meaning . . .

Over time, they listened . . . to the ancient stories of Trickster, or the personal experience stories of the adults and elders that showed what can happen in a ceremony, or in a sacred gathering, when the meanings and good intentions turn discordant. They learned to be patient, with others and with themselves. They learned there are no quick fixes to wisdom, or even when it comes to healing. They listened to the stories. To the narratives. They contemplated their significance, their relevance. They listened to the stories when the spirit drumming taps the Spirit of all that is and nourishes the Spirit of all who are present, and how the energy can become so strong, it can alter time and perception, and make things happen that are good.

Whether a ceremony of a hundred, or a ceremony of one, the intention of the moment reconnects us to the Spirit within us that is in all things, and to the Great Holy Mystery, and it is from that place the spirit drumming begins.

Within the stories of these journeys dwell the teachings. The lessons. The way to be and perhaps not to be . . . The choices we have been given. What I have learned, as little as that may be, and what the writers in *Spirit Drumming* have contributed from their own life journeys and the drum, we share with you—the feelings, the situations, the wisdom, and even the magic that exists within them. The rest is up to you.

And so, as it was then, may it be now . . .

THE DRUMMING OF THE ELDERS
MariJo Moore

The spirit of the wind shook the trees
as if wanting them to leave
and not witness what was to happen.

But the trees felt the drumming
beating deep inside their roots
and accepted the bliss of needful pain.

They heard the pounding of their brothers
making known the sadness, making known the truth
awakening the stagnant message of old.

Reminding the trees, as they had always known
before healings can occur, hurt has to be drummed out
and acknowledged and accepted.

The elders cried with worry of their grandchildren
tears falling onto the resonant skins, drumming, drumming
repeating fears that the world is changing.

But the pain carried in the drumbeats
is necessary to reach the hearts of the young
and allow them to accept the knowledge of the elders.

The world is changing but old ways can be modernized.
This is the way of growth.
Message given, message carried, message received.

The drums have done their part
the trees have witnessed and blessed the sounds
and the spirit of the wind is at rest.
—MARIJO MOORE, INDIGENOUS AUTHOR, POET, EDITOR, SEER;
EDITOR OF *GENOCIDE OF THE MIND* AND *WHEN SPIRITS VISIT*.

CHAPTER TWO

ON THE BACK OF A TURTLE'S SHELL

Through this Native American creation account, a story reveals less about the creation of the universe, but does, however, reveal a lot about how humankind is descended from the stars, from the people who live in the Sky. That's how it was explained to me. As humans, everything that we are created from is of the Earth, our Mother. But, the origin of our existence, the ones who created us, who made us, descended from the Sky People, the first immigrants. What this creation account also reveals in its telling is that we all come from Woman . . .

Imagine the turtle drum beating now; the heart of a turtle often beats long after the turtle has died. Turtles are known for their strong hearts, so a turtle drum, even one made of wood and animal skin with turtle symbols, especially resonates with the heart of the Earth and the hearts of all beings. There are still Indigenous peoples of North America who call this land Turtle Island. Or Turtle Continent. And one reason for this is the stories that are passed on, not just through listening or reading, but those stories felt in the blood . . .

Listen as the turtle drum speaks . . .

Ages ago, before there were people in the world, Mother Earth was covered in water. It has been said that there were no people living in the world at this time. They lived in the Sky World, and that it was from this world that the ancestors of humans had arrived on Mother Earth . . .

A woman fell from the stars through a hole in the Sky World where she had lived. The hole opened into this world, which was then all water, on which floated waterfowl of many kinds. There was no land at that time. It came to pass that as these waterfowl saw this young woman falling, they shouted, "Let us receive her," whereupon they—at least some of them—joined their bodies together, and the young woman fell on this platform of bodies. When these grew weary, they asked, "Who will volunteer to care for this woman?" The great turtle then took her, and when he got tired of holding her, he in turn asked who would take his place.

At last the question arose as to what they should do to provide her with a permanent resting place in this world. Finally, it was decided to prepare the Earth on which she would live in the future. To do this it was determined that soil from the bottom of the primal sea should be brought up and placed on the broad, firm carapace of the turtle, where the shell would increase in size to such an extent that it could accommodate Sky Woman and all the creatures that would be produced on land thereafter. After much discussion, the toad was finally persuaded to dive to the bottom of the waters in search of soil. Bravely making the attempt, he succeeded in bringing up soil from the depths of the sea. This was carefully spread over the carapace of the turtle, and at once both began to grow in size and depth.

After the young woman recovered from her fall from the upper world, she built herself a shelter, in which she lived quite contentedly. In the course of time she brought forth a girl baby, who grew rapidly in size and intelligence . . . The daughter then gave birth to male twins who had the power to change the world—changes that would make living on Earth for all beings a pursuit of balance within an easy and comfortable life, and a life of struggle and challenge.

And thus life on land began on the back of a great turtle, and a woman who fell from the Sky.

CHAPTER THREE

IN THE LAND OF THE DRUM

The way things are going in the world right now, the power of what is bad seems to be making everything out of balance and, the way I see it, we're hanging on to this out-of-balance world by a thread, and that thread has connected us to this book. That thread has connected us to the drum.

The times we live in are very different from the ones when tribal drums resounded throughout this land. Yes, just as we do today, the ancients certainly had their challenges. I have learned from various tribal peoples of this land, that this is not the First World, nor even the Second. We are living, according to some of them, in the Fourth World. For others, the Fifth World. And I have learned that those in each world met with great changes. For some of us, as for those who lived in past worlds, a certain despair suffuses our planet and all beings who separate their hearts from the Earth. The beating in our hearts is the beating in hers. The beating of the drum is our thread intertwining with the pulse of the Mystery. It may very well be the sound of our new emergence into the next world.

I understand that today on Turtle Island, in this land of the drum, civilized humans have intellectually separated themselves from nature, causing cataclysmic changes for much of life on Mother Earth. So many people have become so civilized in their thinking, and surrounded by so many technologies, that they have embraced the oh-so-silly idea that because they have these technologies, they are the planet's superior beings. This self-proclaimed superiority has given them the freedom to be irresponsible in dealing with our environment, as well as violent and oppressive toward each other and all other life forms. This is not the mentality that Sky Woman perceived as she was rescued by the beings who lived here. It is not the kind of mentality I would want to bring to the drum and to my drumming.

So this is my advice of nearly seventy years on this journey: Hold on to that thread that has led you to the drum as if it were tethered to your very soul and spirit. You see, regardless of all the technology at our fingertips, some of us still have a semblance, a speck of primal spirit that beckons, that hasn't been so diluted that it has disappeared. No matter where we originated, many of us have felt the power of this land of the drum and have been drawn to that which is ancient.

That being said, this continued interest in the drum might also be one of civilized society's passing whims, an attempt by some merely to try something new. It may be fun. It may be exhilarating. It may momentarily satisfy that feeling we have of wanting to reconnect to something tribal. But, for others, perhaps even many, using a drum for expression of spirit, using a drum to pray, or using a drum to connect with something sacred may very well be what they truly need, but not what they really want. No one is looking up at you from these pages and judging.

On the other hand, this idea of the drum could be a newfound passion, which now emerges from somewhere deep inside you; an enchanting curiosity, perhaps, that summons you, and does offer you wisdom that can help to guide you, magic that can help you secure your hold to the Earth, energy your soul has been crying out for. Maybe that is why the drum is beckoning you.

And so, now may be the time, or not, to decide that when you hold the drum, and beat upon the skin of a living being, you are connecting to an ancient way of feeling life on this land called Turtle Island. Of seeing life on this land. Of living life as it was originally intended in the land of the drum—and all the while listening to the beating that is your own heart.

MY SENSES ON FIRE

Lisa Davis

I first heard it at the Red School House in St. Paul, Minnesota, many decades ago.

It was so powerful and loud! My senses were on fire—I viscerally felt "it" in my body. Felt what? I didn't really know. It was indescribable and ineffable. The collective drumbeats, mixed with the voices in different octaves, entranced me. I felt as if I was being hugged in the metaphorical arms of a loving mother (Mother Earth!). The rhythms and tones were hypnotic.

As a Red School House student, and the only non-Native student to have graduated from there, I was honored to be invited to sing with their drum group. I got to experience a deep tradition steeped in the centuries. I am eternally grateful; it was a rich experience on so many levels. With the drum, I felt connected to everyone and everything. The drum took me out of my head and into my heart and spirit. I felt the circle *in* me. Not just the feeling of being part of the circle, but the circle itself. For me, it was a direct conduit to God, the Creator, and the Great Mystery. As a teenager who suffered much chaos and confusion, this place offered beauty, comfort, and safety. The voices and the drumbeats would float above any earthly worries. Hearing that, I knew we all belonged and I felt the compassionate respect for every being—be it person, animal, bird, tree, or stone.

Recently, I visited the northern Minnesota woods. I was on a hundred-acre farm, with sixty acres in its native forest. Walking through the forest alone, I felt the intangible presence of the drum circle. Spontaneously, I started using my hand as a drumstick. Instantly, I burst out into a Native song. I may have made it up but I felt the presence of the collective spirits around me. For the next few days, I sang this song over and over again, sometimes at the top of my lungs. The pulse of the rhythm helped remind me that I am part of the circle and I am the circle itself.

—LISA DAVIS, LABORATORY SCIENTIST AND PSYCHOTHERAPIST,
1975 GRADUATE OF RED SCHOOL HOUSE.

CHAPTER FOUR

ANOTHER WAY OF SEEING . . . THE HOLY LAND

The people living in this land now, a land that many Indigenous peoples today still refer to as Turtle Island, do not regard anywhere in the Americas as the Holy Land. For them, the Holy Land exists in the Middle East, or some other place in the world. However, the Holy Land for me, and many of the peoples represented in this book, remains here, in the place more commonly to all of us known as America.

This does not mean we cannot have more than one Holy Land because the Earth herself is holy. She is sacred.

We can never be free of violence in this country until the people who live in this country regard the very land they walk upon as their Mother.

—NIPPAWANOCK

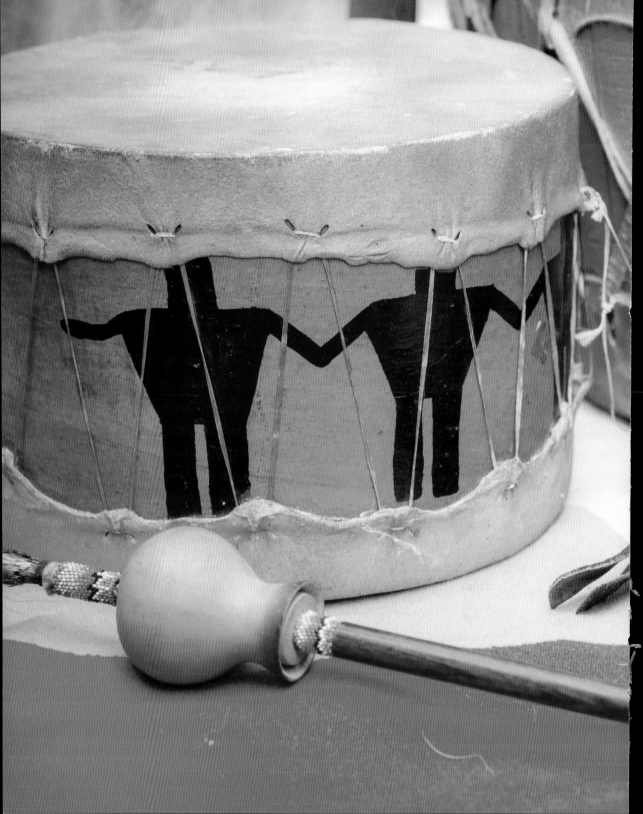

PART TWO

BIRTH AND REBIRTH

Rebirth of an Indigenous Kind

It's like we've gone through a different sort of maturation, a process of spiritual growth,
however slow or intense,

and we evolve back to a higher state of primal state of mind,

an insightful awareness of our place,

a deeper consciousness, and we change

seeing ourselves in the world that is never quite the same . . .

We have been Reborn into Nature! And, for many of us, it can be the
sound of the beating drum

that initiates our rebirth, our reconnection . . . That exists within our own hearts

And brings us home.

CHAPTER FIVE

BECAUSE WE USE THE DRUM

What can be more precious than a newborn child being introduced to the universe? For me, nothing. To beat the drum to help prepare the path of words to come: to hold that baby up to the Sky, to turn that baby to the four directions, to lift that baby into the embrace of nature, introducing the infant to all things great and small. I have asked through prayerful petition that the forces of life and nature allow this new person passage through the stages of life and into the sacred time of old age. What can be more important? What can be more symbolic? What could be more meaningful?

For me, nothing.

The way of the drum takes us to these special moments. Because we use the drum, we acknowledge our relatives of Earth and Sky. Because we use the drum, we see ourselves as a part of this incredible world and unimaginable universe. Because we use the drum, our children and our grandchildren will know that their part in creation began here and now with their introduction to the universe.

Or, perhaps, it is your own introduction. Perhaps it is you who has the need to stand on our Mother, the Earth, beneath our Father, the Sky, and introduce yourself to them. Tell them and the Moon and the Sun and stars, and the clouds and the wind, and the rain and the waters of the Earth, and the birds and the animals, tell all the life you feel and see around you . . . Tell them who you are—a relative who lives among them! Ask for their permission . . .

A PRAYER PRESENTING AN INFANT TO THE WORLD

[The drum, the one that you care for, the drum where you leave your tobacco offerings, burn your prayer sage, or purify with your sweetgrass. Now, even in your mind, this, the drum you begin beating, beating steady, a strong steady rhythm . . .]

Ho! You Sun, Moon, Stars [say the words]
All you that move in the heavens,
I bid you hear me!

[The drum still beating steady, a strong quiet rhythm you will not stop until the address has been made, appealing to powers and elements of the world, and of the universe.]

Into your midst has come a new life.
Consent you, I implore!
Make his path smooth,
That he may reach the brow of the First Hill!

[The drum still beats steady, strong, now in sync with everything.]

Ho! You winds, clouds, rain, and mist [say the words aloud]
All you that move in the air,
I bid you hear me!
Into your midst has come a new life.
Consent you, I implore! [Drum still steady, still beating . . .]
Make his path smooth,
That he may reach the brow of the Second Hill!

[Drumming . . . Drumming . . . Drumming . . . Steady steady in rhythm with your heart and the heart of Earth and the origin of all things . . . steady, beating, steady, beating, beating, beating . . .]

Ho! You hills, valleys, rivers, lakes, ocean, trees, grasses
All you of the Earth [beating, beating, beating . . . speak to them!]
I bid you hear me! [beating, beating, beating . . .]
Into your midst has come a new life.

[Beating steady beating steady strong beating steady strong in rhythm with your heart and the Heart of the Earth and the origin of all things beating steady, steady, beating . . .]

Consent you, I implore!
Make his path smooth,
That he may reach the brow of the Third Hill!

[Still drumming, having not missed a beat. Steady drumming rhythmic drumming. Drumming that connects your heart of words and the Heart of Earth with the origin of all things. Steady, steady, the beating, the energy flowing stronger not diverted and on course, steady into the Mystery . . . the beating of the drum . . .]

Ho! You birds, great and small,
That fly in the air [speak to them, sing to them all!]
Ho! You animals, great and small,
That dwell in the forest,
Ho! You insects that creep among the grasses
And burrow in the ground,
I bid you hear me!

Into your midst has come a new life. [Keep drumming, drumming, drumming]
Consent, consent, I implore!
Make his path smooth,
That he may reach the brow of the Fourth Hill!

[Still beating steady, steady in rhythm with your heart and the Heart of the Earth and the universe . . .]

Ho! All you of the heavens, all you of the air
All you of the Earth,
I bid you hear me!
Into your midst has come a new life.
Consent you, I implore!
Make his path smooth
Then he may travel beyond the Four Hills!

[Drumming, drumming, drumming, drumming . . . fading like the rolling thunder fading like the distant rolling thunder fading fading until you stop.]

CHAPTER SIX

WHEN I FIRST HEARD THE SONG

When I first heard the song introducing me to the universe, *I* was no infant.

I heard that song as the Sun was setting on a Saturday evening in the autumn of 1971, while I was attending the university. We had just finished dinner. We were standing in the backyard of my uncles' house in Tampa. My "godmother," Princess Red Wing, was visiting from Dove Crest, up in Rhode Island. She was there in the circle with us as well as my two uncles, whom I affectionately called Uncle Met and Uncle Nip. Uncle Nip had just used the sharp edge of a small knife to cut a forefinger on each of our hands until they bled. We held them over the center of the circle and mixed our blood together. We were family in a way that nothing could be more sacred. We were part of a tribe. But the song introducing me to the universe would come later in the ceremony before I received my Indian name . . . Imagine the presence of the sacred pipe. Imagine the drumming of Princess Red Wing as we faced each direction. Four times the beat on the woman's drum. I can imagine it now . . .

They called my name out to the four directions!
To the East, to the South, to the West, to the North,
and then they called my name out to the Earth
and to the Sky.
They spoke my name aloud to Manitou.
They called my name out to the birds
And to the butterflies.

To the wind and waters and the air.
They called my name:
White Deer, White Deer, White Deer, White Deer, they cried,
Four times,
White Deer is here!

And then the final words of the song . . .
Make his path smooth
That he may reach beyond the Four Hills!

Many years later, and I am almost there . . . beyond the Four Hills preparing as best as I can to be reborn into the Mystery once again.

But, on that day, in my uncles' backyard in Tampa, I experienced my second birth in this lifetime. Fully and wholly Indigenous. No half, no part, no number, no government approval. No proof of how much blood quantum required. No paper required. No "identity card" ever needed. I was Indigenous! A member of the family of Princess Red Wing, Metacomet, and Nippawanock of the Narragansett Tribe/Wampanoag Nation.

But that naming and blood ceremony didn't happen until I had proven myself. My introduction to the universe did not come until I had proven my courage in battle and counted my first coup, showed myself in their eyes to be a man of good heart, worthy of tribal and family initiation, and had been introduced and felt the oneness of the warrior drum. And that required proof of courage, dedication, and value to the people. It would require my intelligence. It would enable me to hear in a way I had never heard before.

My own heart beating . . .

A PART OF THE WORLD AGAIN!

Amy Krout-Horn

Raised outside the rich culture of my Lakota ancestry, I didn't find an existential space where my heart felt at home until my early twenties, when diabetes caused me to go blind, and my life journey took me into the Minneapolis/St. Paul urban American Indian community. My first experience with the drum and the healing power it wields came in the form of the Mystic Lake powwow in Shakopee, a Dakota community south of the Twin Cities. At the time, I was a student at the University of Minnesota and a sighted classmate from my Dakota language course offered me a ride. When we reached Shakopee, she pulled her car into the Mystic Lake Casino's parking lot, where a shuttle would take us to the nearby powwow grounds. As we waited in the warm late afternoon sunshine, I could hear the traffic roaring along the highway and footsteps moving toward and away from the casino entrance. Every time one of the many doors opened, the tinny mechanical cacophony of the slot machines drifted out and reminded me of another visit to this place, a visit that involved losing $20, losing my orientation, and losing my mind just a little as all the external machine noise—bells, whistles, sirens, robotic digital tones mocking all real forms of music—closed in around me and, somehow, made my total blindness feel far more blinding.

Then, in a brief window of odd quiet, where the traffic dwindled and the casino discord was contained, I heard them off in the distance. I heard drums. A few seconds later, the shuttle bus pulled up in front of us, muffling the distant beat, but not before my pulse quickened, my blood answering some ancient call. The shuttle doors swung open, my friend climbed aboard, and I followed, white cane in hand, heart thumping with anticipation.

When the doors opened again, we were a hundred yards or so from the dance and drum circles, and when I stepped off the bus, the drumbeats rushed in around me, some invisible herd of mammoth proportions, carrying me with its force, but without my fear, toward the center. I took my friend's arm and we walked rapidly toward that center, and with each step I took, that center and my center became one. By the time we reached the circle's edge my heart matched the drum's hard, steady rhythm. But it wasn't just the heart. On a deep cellular level, the vibrations seemed to penetrate, connect, shake, fuse, mend, heal, embrace, accept, love. The drum's driving baritone boom, boom, boom and the high piercing voices of the traditional singers untied memories from the strands of my DNA, and sewed back together the recently torn pieces of my soul.

Since losing my sight a few years earlier, I had moved through the world with an alienating sense of exclusion, as if a dark bubble surrounded me. More often than not, the noise of the external world—inner-city traffic, the buzz of conversation in the large college auditoriums, the blaring dance music of the university watering holes, the expansive din of the Mall of America—served as a sort of prison, holding me inside the lightless bubble, reminding me that I would never again fully be a part of that external space beyond. But unlike those auditory taunts of the modern urban environment, the sounds of the *wacipi*, the powwow, burst through that cursed, confining bubble. Wind surged through a metallic forest; the jingle dress dancers' regalia tinkled; bells rang from the ankles and wrists of powerful, agile young men; the singers' cries rose and fell, all in perfect union with the drum, the beautiful pulse of Mother Earth, the voice of *Wakan Tanka*, the Great Mystery. Open, freed, weeping, I let it all wash over me, through me, until my darkness was cleansed away, and for the first time, in a very long time, I felt pure, I felt whole, I felt alive.

—AMY KROUT-HORN, NATIONAL AWARD–WINNING COAUTHOR OF *TRANSCENDENCE* AND AUTHOR OF *MY FATHER'S BLOOD* AND *DANCING IN CONCRETE MOCCASINS*.

PART THREE

THE ORIGIN

For after all the great religions

have been revealed by brilliant scholars,

or have been written in books and embellished in fine language with finer covers,

man—all mankind—is still confronted with

the Great Mystery.

—LUTHER STANDING BEAR (DAKOTA)

The original attitude of the American Indian toward the Eternal, the "Great Mystery" that surrounds and embraces us, was as simple as it was exalted. To him it was the supreme conception, bringing with it the fullest measure of joy and satisfaction possible in this life.

—OHIYESA (DAKOTA) FROM *THE SOUL OF THE INDIAN*

Wah'kon~tah is the sum total of all things, the collective totality that always was— without beginning, without end. Neither a force nor a spirit, it is the inexplicable sharing-togetherness that makes all things . . . their forms collectively creating the form of Wah'kon~tah which is, obviously, incapable of being anthropomorphized.

—THOMAS E. SANDERS (NIPPAWANOCK)

CHAPTER SEVEN

THE GREAT HOLY MYSTERY

I stood alongside my motorcycle outside of the house in the driveway looking up at the stars. Orion was clearly visible. Even each of the Seven Sisters, the Pleiades, could be seen. The silver of those stars, and the silver and seventies-fashioned hair of my two loving uncles, glistened in the darkness. Fluorescent. Luminous. I don't recall who spoke, but one of us commented at how many stars there were and how "especially bright they seemed tonight." Funny, I didn't think of it back then, but my two uncles were named for stars. Nippawanock, Star that Rises to Greet the Dawn, and Metacomet, Shooting Star. And, in the Pilgrim tradition of Kings and Queens encountering the Narragansetts and Wampanoag, some 500 years ago, they were princes as well.

"Do you still think there is some Divine man up there looking out for you, Gabriel?" My heart started drumming. Uncle Nip smiled. He was referring to a conversation that took place over dinner . . .

Our understanding of everything sprang from the Great Mystery. This is what I learned about being Indigenous. About being Indian. About being Native. About becoming a human being. Through this understanding I could see how vibration, songs, and drums worked their influences and even their magic, which, when you break it down in civilized thinking, is simply science.

"The Great Mystery is in all things, Nephew. If that's what you're asking."

I nodded.

We had been sitting at the round table in the den by the fireplace. "Now, could you pass me your glass?" He poured me some soda. Then, looking up at his brother, asked if he would like another . . . Uncle Met placed the can of Old Milwaukee alongside his dinner plate, his hand waved once over it, and he shook his head. "I'm good."

His brother, my Uncle Nip, glanced at me and then picked up his fork. "And all things are in the Mystery, Gabriel, making everything of equal importance and consequence."

I felt the beating of my heart, and for the first time it sounded for me like a drum.

We ate the delicious stew and drank as I contemplated the lesson in what scholars at the university were referring to now as quantum physics.

"The Great Mystery always was, and will always be," he continued. "We cannot comprehend this as human beings. We are not capable. But the result is our awareness that we are connected to all things because all things are of the Mystery. We are part of a Totality that always was, and will always be. A sharing-togetherness, if you like. A Oneness which cannot be anthropomorphized into a male God with a personal interest in your life . . ."

He buttered a piece of cornbread. I was still quite aware of the drumming in my heart. "Trust me, Nephew, the people didn't aspire to be great people out of fear of going to hell, or out of the hope of living forever inside the pearly gates in an afterlife happy hunting ground."

He sipped his decaf. "If it weren't for the hard work of certain individuals who sacrificed themselves for the benefit of the people, and even a bit of supernatural intervention, our ancestors never would've attained what they did. Deganawida and Hyonwatha could never have created the Law of Great Peace. Tecumtha would not have formed the confederacy at Tippecanoe. The architecture of the Anasazi would not have been created. The Maya and Aztec would not have built their great libraries. We wouldn't be healthy today eating the foods first planted at Machu Picchu, or in the gardens of the Wampanoag . . .

"It was all done without the assistance of capital G-o-d. They were accomplishments of a people who understood . . . they were responsible for their lives and their interactions with all others. They understood that they were interrelated to all things in a cosmic Totality too great to imagine."

I was eating and thinking and listening. And then I asked, "What about the Great Spirit?" I had heard the reference used often by Indians and non-Indians. "Is that the Great Mystery?"

"Among the elders who still speak their Native languages, the idea is that everything has spirit, and the sum total of all spirit is the Great Spirit, then that can be understood as similar. But in English, you see, spirit has a definition. It is defined. Thus, it's still attempting, consciously or not, to define what is unknown and mysterious."

"What about the Creator?" I had often heard both terms used.

"Which creator?" he said and smiled. "Among our people, some record various creators and creatresses. Trickster was a Creator. The Earth is Creatress. What about Spider Grandmother of the Hopi? Just as by definition of a god, as being supernatural and immortal, the angels in Catholicism are gods. Including Lucifer. When our people speak of the First Cause as Creator, there exists a tendency to still retain a mesh of the Judeo-Christian and the Indian. Creator is still assigning the male gender to the First Cause, not much different than capital G-o-d, though I know when we hear our people use that term, they are speaking English, and let's face it, English is a foreign language . . ."

He smiled again and took the last forkful of stew. Uncle Met tilted the can to his lips and sat back in his chair.

"It's all about how we as individuals have been taught, Gabriel, and the elders who knew these things, these concepts, were often translated biasedly by priests and missionaries and anthropologists, or in their own translations into English, were not clear and specific enough . . .

"We're just grateful they got translated at all, or so much more would've been lost."

I picked up the dishes and placed them on the kitchen counter, my Uncle Nip running dishwater at the sink. "What about the people who believe in God?" I asked.

"Then God exists for them," he answered. "For He is, like all things, a part of the Great Mystery."

We stood, the three of us in the driveway. Uncle Nip was smiling again, this time in a way that could make a person either want to flee from embarrassment, or smile too. I was smiling. My Uncle Met was looking at me as well, and like the teacher he was, saying in silence, *You got this, kid.* The stars gleamed above in an endless satin sky. Uncle Nip observed my scanning the night. "You imagine *Him* now up there," he said, "thinking, *Hmm . . . What can I do for Gabriel today?*"

The drum that was now my heart pounded again. *Why is it so hard to let go?* They understood. *I got it.* But my heart was pounding. I could *feel* the sound inside me. Was it fear that evoked such response? Was it excitement at the moment of enlightenment? Was it my tribal reconnection, my conscious awareness?

I shook my head, and scoffed like a young boy. "No," I responded. "I don't think *He's* up there paying particular interest to me, or any of this." But the sense of abandonment became a sudden reality as I uttered those words.

My uncles, however, had long perceived this coming.

"There is Wah-kon-tah," he said. It was an Omaha name he often used for the Great Holy Mystery. I could tell he loved the sound. "And Wah-kon-tah is everything. That means you, kid. That means God, too."

My heart pounded, a drum signaling the spirit of Orenda, something he had described once to me as the spiritual power of one's people, that collective awareness William Butler Yeats called *spiritus mundi*, Carl Jung called the collective unconscious, and Sigmund Freud called racial memory. And with each beat of the drum that was my heart I felt more coherent, more aware and conscious, than I ever had before.

· · · · · · · · ·

I mean, if we consider the idea that we all may come from a tribal past, it is no wonder we are drawn to these ancient philosophies, and to these things like the drum that call us back in time when Earth was Mother, when everything was related. Or maybe we have evolved to this higher state of consciousness, led by the teachings of those who still retained them, those who have not forgotten . . .

At that moment, standing under the stars in the driveway at my uncles' house, I forever let go of that concept of an almighty male God that the Catholic church—and our society—had programmed into my child's brain. This was my liberation from the anthropomorphic belief in a First Cause, and my absolute acceptance of an Indigenous identity that would take me on a journey, and would one day allow me to beat upon the drum and call myself a human being.

This anecdote of a life experience is not intended to demean anyone's religious belief, or spiritual perceptions. It's simply to help you understand where I learned that spirit drumming had originated, from the kind of thought-process that came to us as human beings. For me, staying true to this concept of the Great Mystery was the only way I could use a drum. It was the spiritual understanding given to me and how I received it. We all have our own paths to walk. We ourselves must walk the path.

I looked at my Uncle Nip, that night we stood in the driveway together, and nodded. "Yes," I said. "Yes. I do understand what you're saying about the Great Holy Mystery . . ."

"Gabriel, you may battle the indoctrination your whole life because that's what indoctrination does."

My Uncle Met, standing silent behind his brother, holding a beer at his side, lowered his head. His concentrated gaze on the stars and space and time had quickly readjusted back to me. He didn't need to speak. He rarely did. Facial expressions and gestures often spoke without his voice. I could hear my heart again. I could feel the drum inside me again.

I snapped on my motorcycle helmet with the upside-down American flag on one side, peace sign on the other, Indian design on the back, and got on my bike and lifted the kickstand. "Thanks for dinner," I said. "I'll see you at the university tomorrow, Uncle." I peeked behind him. "See you later, Uncle Met." I pressed the starter button, and the 450 ccs rumbled beneath me, its energy I imagined like a stallion ready to run.

Nip put his hand on my shoulder, my Uncle Met still in silence, alongside him now. "Things are going to change, Nephew." When he spoke those words, I could see the blue intensity in his eyes that I had learned to recognize over the years as very serious.

"The changes coming to the Earth will be great . . . You may live to see some of them." He was speaking with a deep sense of knowing, a kind of knowing not to be questioned. "But your children will see them, and their children."

I sensed my drum-beating heart again, as if the beating were aligned with the Earth herself, actually originating from the Earth in that moment. Even from the universe. It was almost too big for my chest. I could feel it with the bike's engine rumbling, I could feel it . . . Changes . . . Changes to Earth and Sky . . . *My children?* I thought. *My children's children?*

As I drove off into the darkness, my two uncles, for just a moment, seemed like ghosts, maybe even spirits, as they appeared in the bike's rearview mirror. They were talking, and turning toward the house, and then they faded away . . . *Future ghosts*, I heard him say once. That we can sometimes see . . .

Even as I lay in bed with my black Lab E on the throw rug alongside me that night, I fell asleep to the sound of the drum that was my beating heart. It had been there all through dinner. All through our talk in the driveway. I'd feel it over the motorcycle's engine on the ride home. The beating. The pounding in my chest. And I fell asleep aware of the sound of my beating heart.

CHAPTER EIGHT

RECONNECTING MYSELF TO THE THREAD

So, holding the hand drum on my knee now, with my stick in the other hand, I close my eyes and beat until the steady conscious rhythm emerges, a bit faster and softer than the one I felt that night when my Indian uncles helped me reconnect in appreciation to my relationship to All That Is. I sing the Narragansett-Wampanoag name that my godmother, Princess Red Wing, sang for the Great Mystery. And with the beating of the drum, I sing . . .

A SONG TO THE MYSTERY

All is sacred.

All is beautiful.

All is Manitou.

Way hey, way hey ya, way hey ya ha, way hey ya . . .

Beauty is before me.

Beauty is behind me.

Beauty is around me.

Beauty is within me.

Manitou is beauty.

Manitou . . . Great Mystery.

Way hey, way hey ya, way hey ya ha, way hey ya . . .

Sky is beauty.

Clouds are beauty.

Earth is beauty.

Sun is beauty.

Moon is beauty.

Stars are beauty.

Manitou is beauty.

Manitou . . . Great Mystery.

Way hey, way hey ya, way hey ya ha, way hey ya . . .

Mountains are beauty.

Prairies are beauty.

Deserts are beauty.

Forests are beauty.

Manitou is beauty.

Manitou . . . Great Mystery . . .

Way hey, way hey ya, way hey ya ha, way hey ya . . .

Rivers are beauty.

Oceans are beauty.

Water is beauty.

Manitou is beauty.

Manitou . . . Great Mystery . . .

Way hey, way hey ya, way hey ya ha, way hey ya . . .
Deer are beauty.
Buffalo are beauty.
Wolves are beauty.
Bears are beauty.
Animals are beauty.
Fish and crabs are beauty.
Dolphins are beauty.
Whales are beauty.
Birds and bees are beauty.
Butterflies are beauty.
Manitou is beauty.
Manitou . . . Great Mystery . . .

Way hey, way hey ya, way hey ya ha, way hey ya . . .
All is sacred.
All is beautiful.
All is Manitou . . .
Way hey, way hey ya, way hey ya ha, way hey ya . . .

CHAPTER NINE

LIFE EXPERIENCES, THE WAY OF THE DRUM

When I beat on the drum, I beat for power, for strength, and for life. I beat for healing, insight, and wisdom. I beat the drum for sustenance, for rain, and for sun. For celebration and happiness. I beat out of grief and gratitude. I beat for honoring. I beat out of love and loss, and I beat the drum because it is Indigenous power. I do not drum without a conscious awareness of myself in the Mystery, and without loving the Earth as my Mother . . .

For I have come to understand, and have learned, that this is the way of the drum.

But I am not you. Your experiences may be similar to mine, or very different. And yet, we do share the human condition, and that condition proceeds from the same source that, to my understanding, is the Great Mystery.

Are we not each on a journey to try to understand ourselves? Do we not seek through books, like this one, some kind of connection, some kind of guidance to help us walk this journey? Even an affirmation that we are not alone. I have learned from elders, from children, and from my students. I have learned from history and through experience. And I have learned so much through books. My uncles used to tell me not to scoff if I read something I didn't like, or even if I read an entire book I didn't like. "Because," they said, "there is some good in each."

What I envision as the way of the drum is all I have learned. It is up to each of us to determine if any of this makes sense.

CHAPTER TEN

THE MYSTERY

The transcendental movement in the United States was an eighteenth-century philosophical and literary movement spearheaded by a few well-known American poets and writers, in particular. They had come closer than other European descendants on the American continent to the concept of Oneness, or Totality, that the Indigenous people of the Americas had understood, regarding our relationship to nature and to the universe. American literature produced at that time by the likes of Emerson, Whitman, Thoreau, and Dickinson was collectively, and curiously, regarded historically as the Age of Enlightenment. It is, however, unfortunate that their most poignant pieces regarding the relationship between humans and nature, and humans and the universe have all but been censored from American public and private schools, or at best, only casually referenced. As a teacher in the public school system, I saw firsthand, little by little, year by year, the literature disappeared.

In one of his most widely known poems of the 1960s, Ralph Waldo Emerson writes of Brahma, assuming the speaker as Brahma, the Hindu concept of the collective soul, the Oneness of the universe:

> *Far or forgot to me is near . . .*
> *Shadow and sunlight are the same;*
> *The vanished gods to me appear;*
> *And one to me are shame and fame.*

They reckon ill who leave me out;
When me they fly, I am the wings
I am the doubter and the doubt,
And I the hymn the Brahmin sings.

Brahma is not a Supreme Being, separated from self, separated from nature, existing somewhere separate from the universe. No more than the Great Mystery, Wakan Tanka, can be regarded as a Supreme Being. Everything is Wakan Tanka, and Wakan Tanka is everything.

At the center of the universe dwells Wakan Tanka, and that center is everywhere. It is within each of us . . .

—BLACK ELK (LAKOTA)

Emerson's poem conveys the notion that without this collective sense of Oneness with all things, a human being cannot learn and live with enlightenment.

In a similar spiritual context, Black Elk felt that a human being could only attain "real peace" with a conscious understanding of Wakan Tanka at the center of all things.

As Judaism, Christianity, and Islam encouraged their practitioners to believe in a Supreme and Almighty God apart from human beings, separate from nature, a God who resembles a man, we might ask, after centuries of war and violence against humanity and the environment, *How's that working?*

As NASA research scientists and scientists from other industrialized nations continue to seek life elsewhere in the universe, they objectify life on our living Mother Earth. We might wonder with each hole they blast through the ozone, *How's that going?*

Like my predecessors from more primal and conscious philosophies of the world who understood the concept of Oneness and Totality, I had learned that the First Cause of All Things is not a Supreme Being, but *all* beings, and *all* things collectively living together at the same time.

The idea that a Supreme Being does not sit atop a hierarchy, and that life was not created, nor does it function, as a hierarchy was something that the great mind of Albert Einstein recognized. Like Indigenous thought and ancient wisdom, Einstein also regarded everything as equal because everything made up the whole in the collective totality that is the universe. Organized religions invented the hierarchy of life, a model that Einstein reassessed. Sadly, Western scientists rarely give much weight to Einstein's reassessment. As an example, these scientists came up with the idea of a "food chain." Such a concept has the low resonance of something hard and cold, more technological in its connotations of a "chain." Contrast the civilized concept of a "food chain" with the Indigenous, or primal, view of the Earth's bounty as a web of life, strong and beautiful, and delicate as well. Or like the Earth we live on, moving and turning in a circle of life.

So, whether NASA scientists want to search for life in the clouds of Venus or on the dark side of the Moon or in the canyons of Mars or beneath the frozen ocean of Jupiter's Europa or in the "habitable zone" far out in space on the planet Kepler 186f, they are missing the major point established long ago in more primal and spiritual and less technological ways: Life is everywhere. Life is the Moon and life is Mars and life is Europa, and life is Venus. And life is that distant planet some 490 light-years away that resembles Earth.

Yes, they agree, *in order for life to exist in the universe, there must be water.*

But, water is life, too! Listen to the beating of a water drum in ceremony, and you know that water is alive. Water feels and reacts. And follow the water birds with the spirit within you, and you will find enlightenment . . . Or, just sit on the shore and feel and hear the waves as they break toward you, the rhythm synchronizing with your heart that becomes like a water drum.

Unfortunately, the objectification of life that is water, through organized religious dogma and Western science, allows human beings to disrespect and abuse the very life without which we cannot exist. And in a sad irony, these very people are the ones who regard themselves as *superior* life forms on this planet.

The narrator of Emerson's poem is Brahma, and in a philosophical sense, this is true; the narrator is Brahma, for Brahma is in all things. It is the concept of Oneness. "Brahma is the doubter and the doubt," even "the hymn the Brahmin sings," and even the songs we sing on the drum, or the sound of the beating we make on the drum . . . Even we are part of the Great Holy Mystery.

Everything exists within the Great Mystery, and everything is all at once the Great Mystery, always was, always is, always will be . . . I would ask myself, How could I be a teacher of the people, or make the sacrifice of seeking a vision, or walk the path of the heart, and not feel at the very core of my being that I am a part of an incomprehensible Totality that always was, and will always be? How could I drum and sing the prayers, the songs, the chants without my awareness of the Great Mystery?

The answer, of course, is I could not.

CHAPTER ELEVEN

WISDOM

The quest and seeking of wisdom does not come without a price; and often that price comes in the form of some kind of sacrifice.

There is the song, the singer, the drum, the incantation, and faith, and the rain comes. The clouds part. The mind becomes clear. The body heals. The dreams come. The vision occurs. But, often it cannot happen without sacrifice. For sacrifice is giving that which we hold dear. We may think it can be money, or material objects, and in some ways this can be a source of sacrifice, but it has been said that the only thing we come close to truly owning in our lifetimes is the body where our spirit dwells, where our consciousness exists.

And so, the idea of physically suffering is giving the energy of the body, so others may live, so that the source of energy can be replenished, like a quiet pool that provided us with water. A spirit pool provides us with spirit. If we dip our cups in the pool to sustain ourselves, and each person keeps taking cups for sustenance, the pool will become depleted. That is why we have to fill our cups with goodness, so we can pour that back into the pool of spirit so that others and future generations can have enough. So that future generations will be born with a "spirit-knowing," and they will understand innately how to live on the Earth as originally instructed. In today's world, I have noticed in my own lifetime that so many human eyes seem absent of that spirit-knowing, even among the children. And also, the energy we return to that spirit pool, now ocean, provides energy for that which sustains us, including the Earth, the ocean, the Sky, the Moon, the Sun, and even the stars.

By drumming, we are using our bodies, but only to become more aware of the soul, the spirit, our consciousness, so that we don't forget we are more than body, more than our physical selves.

Replenishing the energy of life on Earth helps one's people and helps the world. Those who are always sapping the Earth of energy—the less evolved of our species who do little but take and take and take, and give nothing back—assume this is their right. But what do we give back? What do we give in return? We can return energy to the Earth, to the Moon, to the Sun, to the Sky, and to all things through our actions, giving back that energy in the form of acts of love and kindness and generosity. We can give back the energy we take to sustain ourselves by creating, whether that be a new life, a work of art, or a poem, a book, a photograph, or a beautiful piece of beadwork . . .

In some instances, an artist will create a pipe for someone to trade or purchase to give that person a way of spiritual expression. An artist will create a rattle, which can often been effective in driving off and decimating negative energy, or spirits not inclined to be helpful and good. An artist can fashion a drum, which has the power, as I have learned and understood it, to summon the spirit of the ancestors. I learned that the ancestors expected human art to mimic the creation; therefore, it should be the very best of what a human could manifest and contribute.

We can often, by the very path we walk, learn to give back, and oftentimes this return will involve sacrifice. We can even return morsels of that energy when we drum for life!

I was taught, and grew to understand, that what we require to live and be healthy and happy, will not happen without sacrifice, and certainly not without respect and gratitude.

Some chanting and drumming goes on and on and on throughout a night. I have wondered at these times if my arm would be capable of such endurance. Would my hands cramp and not allow me to continue? And not always does the Power work as we hope.

I have sung and drummed to save lives, and not all those I sang and drummed for lived. I sang and drummed for those who have died. I sang to attract someone who should not have been with me, and the Power did not work. The vibration was not right. Still, each time I drum and chant and use the drum for incantation, I have faith that it will work if the vibrations I am sending forth are accepted, or maybe the right ones. I'm not going to fool the Mystery. If you can understand the scientific principle of vibration and the law of attraction, then you can understand, to some extent, how it works. But to experience the sacred song and the drum together is to feel it when the magic does manifest, and it does work.

Few can say it is easy to let go of years of early childhood indoctrination.

When we do let things go that are no longer useful, if it is right, and we are in the proper state of mind, we will come across other things on our paths, things that will help us carry on. For me, these were the Indigenous things. They were of the Earth, my Mother, and Sky, my Father. They came from the water, Mother Ocean. Any void left from abandoning institutionalized religious dogma got filled with the Indigenous ideas and perspectives of life, the most important being the concept of the Great Holy Mystery. As a child, you might say, I sacrificed the rosary beads, and later in my process of maturation, and becoming a teacher, I picked up the round stones. I sacrificed the symbol of the cross I was taught to worship as a boy, and was introduced to the symbols in nature, and then to the sacred pipe as a young man. Even the songs of Christian salvation—now gone—I've sacrificed before the chants and the beating of the drum.

CHAPTER TWELVE
THE OPPOSITION

And so, back then, when I was finding the words to give meaning to the way I was feeling, I was ready to learn about living the way of the drum on the path of a human being.

While I was attending the university, my intention was to become a teacher for the youth of the people. But, how could I teach and provide insight to the literature of the people, which included the chants and songs of the people, the Trickster stories, the great orations, without a conscious awareness of the source of everything there is that makes us human beings, at least as well as I could in this human form? How could I read with them the literature of their own Indigenous creation accounts without the idea of an incomprehensible Totality that always was and forever will be?

How could I teach history if I didn't understand the history of the Americas? If I didn't understand this concept of a Totality, an ineffable Oneness that was trampled upon by the European conquistadors and puritans, and later colonists and settlers, and soldiers and oil tycoons? Missionaries of all kinds, too, were not saving any Indigenous souls, but rather, stealing them, as they still are today. Didn't the current pope, Pope Francis, anoint a man into sainthood who allowed and participated in the brutality and oppression of Indigenous people while operating at least one of these missions in California?

The Europeans' religious vehemence and extremism in the Americas have been romanticized in film and erased from history books and American classrooms, even glorified today in the preservation and maintenance of the missions and the Native American museums. These institutions absolve the Europeans of any responsibility for how they treated the Indigenous peoples, which was undeniably horrific: annihilating entire Native peoples in a physical genocide or usurping their spiritual understanding of themselves in relation to nature and the universe in a cultural genocide. These were the very Native people who sang on the drum and offered sacrifices—energy in the form of vibration—to the Moon and to the Earth and to the Sun. But the first migrations of Europeans to the Americas destroyed all but a few of the great ceremonial mounds; they attempted to destroy, and even buried, the magnificent temples. They smashed the drums. Broke the pipes. They killed with guns and diseases and scorched the Earth in a human and environmental holocaust like no other in the history of human un-kind.

They had to punish the Indigenous people, telling themselves and believing that their anthropomorphic God endorsed this imposed cruelty to enforce His will. They feared the Feathered Serpent. They feared the prophets. They feared the sacrifice at Sundance. They feared the ghost dance. They burned the Mayan and Aztec libraries. They burned the books of wisdom. They forbid spiritual expression. They crushed the great shell mounds, and made them into roads to build their civilization upon. They silenced the drum.

So, my abandonment of this anthropomorphic God concept was crucial to me in becoming a teacher of the people. But the anger welling up inside me for the history once denied me could cloud any vision I would bring to my students in the classroom, whether that classroom was in an old school building, or an auto repair shop, or a prison, or a room in an apartment in the projects, or a basement in a public library, or even in a climate-controlled college classroom equipped with the latest technology.

One day, to deal with this pent-up anger, to confront this bitterness that I did not want to poison my heart, I would be given a chant in a most sacred way. This chant I would sing on the drum to help restore the honor of those descendants who came to the Americas from other parts of the world, and to the descendants of the ones who did the soul-stealing and killing, and even those who are Indigenous today who have forgotten the Great Holy Mystery . . .

PART FOUR

EVERYTHING IS VIBRATION

The echo and

Vibration of the

Drum can be

Heard throughout the world

And the beat

Of our hearts

Resonates with the beat

Of the drum

—A DRUMMER'S QUOTE

PHYSICS

If you want to find the secrets of the universe, think in terms of energy, frequency, and vibration.

—NIKOLA TESLA

Though this statement by Nikola Tesla quietly whispers through the halls of Western science, and also appears to be the ancient philosophy of many Indigenous peoples, a vantage point from which they saw the world and the universe, it is actually pure and simple physics.

PHILOSOPHY

Words have great power. When the ancients said a word spoken has the power to change our form and reality, they understood the idea of frequency and the law of attraction. It is similar to vibration. Raise the energy that we consist of with greater vibration, and attract comparable energy. The frequency and vibration of drumming, accompanied by song, resonates with the Earth, and the universe, and can cause things to happen. It is not only simply physics. It is philosophy.

RESONANCE

Have you ever been scolded or, worse, someone has yelled at you, and belittled you, swore at you, called you stupid, fat, ugly? (You're not really . . .)

Have people ever told you how proud they are of you? How smart you were to do something a particular way! Big difference in the resonance and feelings those words have the power to convey.

Has anyone ever complimented you on how nice you look? How pretty you look when you smile! How handsome you look in your new shirt! "Your garden is so beautiful," I said to my mother-in-law, and saw her smile.

"Thank you," my wife said when I brought her water.

"You are so insightful and helpful," I said to my editor.

Anyone who has experienced the physical and emotional pain and anguish that harsh words can inflict, and the joy and well-being that kind words can engender, knows the power of resonance and frequency. When I pray, I must truly feel that my words have power!

From this awareness, we understand that words are energy. Words are vibrations. Words are sacred. Then why would I choose to use language to manipulate or abuse? This would deplete the level of my vibration, on a scale of one to ten, to a one or a two.

Words raise or lower resonance, and they match the frequency intended. Just listen to the politicians, or the religious zealots. Now introduce a drum into this kind of physics. Is it the beat of soldiers on parade, or the beat of one's heart in tune with the Earth?

CHAPTER THIRTEEN

CHANTING . . .

The great minds of Western science have spoken, and now we can finally agree. Everything is vibration.

In science, in the area of quantum theory, it is taught that when we journey into vibration to the subatomic level, science has now discovered that everything is energy.

This scientific observation holds that the law of vibration serves as the foundation of the law of attraction. Such an idea is at the center of Indigenous wisdom. And so, it is no wonder that a chant on a drum would use vibration to cause something to happen. Chants are incantations using vibrations, and the energies of voice and drum can cause something to happen, even more so at times when dance is included.

This is absolutely understandable—at least, now that science officially gets it.

Over and over again, without missing a beat, every word is sung as it has always been, to cause something to happen. Imagine a whole tribe singing the same incantation for rain. Imagine that the song itself had come from a dream. Imagine that it was, perhaps, of supernatural origin, and radiated the power of a collective voice singing this song. So, of course, Indigenous people could grow corn in the desert. Part clouds in a storm. Divert, or create, a whirlwind. The drums, the singing, the vibration, the energy, the law of attraction, and the awareness of our relationship with all things, and to all things, indeed have the influence to cause something to happen:

Far as we can see,

Comes the rain,

Comes the rain with me . . .

Over the corn,

Over the corn, tall corn,

Comes the rain,

Comes the rain with me . . .

Through the pollen,

Through the pollen blest,

All in pollen hidden,

Comes the rain,

Comes the rain with me . . .

Far as we can see,

Comes the rain,

Comes the rain with me . . .

—EXCERPT FROM A TRIBAL SONG

At the Red School House in St. Paul, back in the seventies, some of the teachers and students would plant a garden by the school. I was a teacher at the time, and I remember the drought, and how the garden was dying. So one day I took the students outside—some of the teachers came, too—and we brought a drum, and sang for rain . . .

We drummed. We sang. And it rained.

I'm not sure how long we spent out there on the dry ground in the thirsty garden, since time, when we speak of it in this context, truly belongs to the Mystery. But I never forgot that feeling, walking back to the school building, nor the image of the little kids running up the steps as the gentle rain fell, and the older students just ahead of me, smiling and talking, and how wondrous it was. I wonder if they remember that chanting moment, the gentle strength of the hand drum's rhythm, and the power in energy, the power in the song, and the conviction that it would happen . . .

Clouds . . .
See the clouds.
Clouds drawing near . . . So lovely . . .
Rain.
See the rain . . .
Rain, people rain!
Rain all around,
Rain falling down . . .
So lovely . . .

Just the singer/drummer pouring his heart out, a communion with nature through song and drum, creating a musical bridge between human and nonhuman. This is a call for rain, the water that provides life. It is a song of coherent awareness, not to an anthropomorphic God living in heaven, but to the very spirit of those beings and energies in nature the singer/drummer/dancer seeks to address. Remember the science: The law of vibration serves as the foundation of the law of attraction. The Mystery is the drum, the sound of the drum, the singer, and the song . . . As all things are of the Mystery, we are each the Mystery in human form and all things in all forms collectively creating the Oneness of the Mystery. Through the beating of the drum, our hearts and the rhythm of the Earth and the universe become synchronized, and cause things to happen.

A SONG SUNG ON A DRUM CAN BE SACRED

A special medicine song, or song of a tribal society, or one belonging to an individual blessed with a dream that brings the song, are sung as flawlessly as possible so as not to create anything but a line of direct communication to that which the drummer/singer is appealing. I remember learning how the AIM song came to the people of the American Indian Movement. How it was passed onto the movement in a traditional way, and how powerful it feels even today when I hear it or sing it. My brother/friend Oannese was a powerful singer and drummer. His wife Betty would often stand behind him and lend her voice to the AIM song. Sometimes, we drummed together, Oannese and me, and sang that song in our home . . . to keep the good spirit of the song alive.

I can recall a time years before that, when I was at a gathering to support a Native man in Tampa who had been fired from his job unjustly. A drum group appeared on the hill in the park. They referred to themselves as "hobbyists." No Indian there denied them the time to sing, but when they began the AIM song, a few Indians walked up the hill and asked them if the hobbyists knew the history about the song they were singing. They looked away and shook their heads. You see, this was the '70s and some Indians were fresh off some difficult times being associated with AIM, and knew friends imprisoned or killed as a result of that association. I had learned at the Heart of the Earth Survival School that it was a tradition, if this song was to be sung, one or two things had to happen. Someone at the drum had to draw blood, and/or someone had to place tobacco on the drum for those who didn't make it. And so, the Indians said to the hobbyists at the gathering, that they could continue singing the song, but first they must make the offering. Next thing, the hobbyists were packing the drum in their van and off they went.

The sound we create with the drum
And the song we sing from a dream . . .
Bridge the world

From the tangible to the intangible,
From the corporeal to the incorporeal,
From the seen to the unseen.

There is the song, the singer, the drum, the incantation, the faith, and even the dance, and the rain comes. But it cannot happen without sacrifice of some kind. For sacrifice is giving something we hold dear to someone else, such as in tribal customs of giveaways, or an individual's suffering through physical pain or challenge and directing that pain to a source that sustains life. And though giveaways, which many tribes practiced, and personal bodily sacrifice were condemned by early colonists and the Catholic Church, the tradition of sacrifice is ironically rooted in the idea of sacrificing one's self for one's country, or for God, or that it was God who sacrificed His son for the sins of Man. In the case of Indigenous sacrifices, it is done personally and individually. It is vibration, almost always accompanied by spiritual drumming, which is returning energy to that energy we need to live and be healthy and happy. I do feel that any changes today in the way we live to help our world's environment and human poverty will not happen without sacrifice, and certainly they won't happen without respect and gratitude.

On some occasions, chanting and drumming goes on throughout a night. I can remember thinking once, *How am I going to last?* And not always does the Power work as we hope, or as we want. If you can understand the principle discovered in science, regarding vibration and the law of attraction, then you can understand in some way, to some extent, how it works. But to experience the sacred song and the drum together is to feel it when the magic, or the science, actually manifests, and it does work. Sun, like the Moon, like the Ocean.

CHAPTER FOURTEEN

A CHANT TO LURE HONOR

Not easy to let go of years of early childhood indoctrination.

When we do let go of material things, beliefs, and ideas that are no longer useful, we may come across other things on our paths, things that will help us carry on. For me, these were the Indigenous things that I call medicine. They were of the Earth, my Mother, and the Sky, my Father. They came from the water, Mother Ocean. They came from the birds and the mammals. Butterflies and dragonflies. And bees and ants. Any void left from abandoning institutionalized religious dogma got filled with the Indigenous ideas and perspectives of life, the most important being the concept of the Great Holy Mystery. I let go of the rosary beads and picked up the round stones. I released the cross and was introduced to the four directions. The book that I was taught was the "word of God" became the pipe that is the word made physical when addressing the Great Mystery. Even the songs of Christian salvation, though still melodically beautiful, became the chants and beating of the drum.

And so, back then, when I was young, I was ready to learn about living the path of a human being. You see, most tribal names can be translated as human beings, or the people. The people of the Flint Nation. The people of the Hills. The people who first greet the dawn. The people where the wind is born. Becoming a human being, though, or becoming what I call myself, an Indigenous man, had always been more than an intellectual choice. No one else could decide this for me. Yes, I chose to walk this path, but that is because this path is what I am.

Besides, at the time of my life when this path was reemerging, not just in me but in many Indigenous peoples of the Americas, I would be graduating from the university, on my way to becoming a teacher. However, my idealism about how I was going to help change the world would not be embraced with open arms and minds. For I understood, to some extent, that teaching in America would be a struggle that would, upon occasion, almost take my life.

HOW AND WHY A CHANT IS BORN

My uncle Nip had taken the warrior's drum out and placed it in the den. This was the Grandfather. He was the same kind of drum that the men of old could have been punished for keeping, a drum men and women were killed for—that and the singing the drum inspired. And yet, the drums, as we know them today in America, were preserved through the bravery of those ancestors, so that the old ways of seeing the world could continue. I feel we should commit to memory their sacrifices, which kept these drums alive, and their power alive, for us to have in our keeping today. Perhaps before any drumming begins, we should offer our gratitude, even with an offering of tobacco in hand and acknowledge those who risked their well-being and even sacrificed their lives so that we would still have these things today.

Though the afternoon sun felt hot outside, inside the darkened den it felt cool. This would be the first time my uncle Nippawanock and I had drummed alone and together. This was the first time I was prepared as a warrior to beat on the warrior's drum. We were getting ready for me to sing "A Chant to Lure Honor."

This chant was a gift to me to lure the hearer to freedom—freedom from the shackles of practices that constrain his spiritual growth, as well as ours, and the civilized behaviors that deny him a sense of honor. So it is a chant to lure the oppressors and to awaken the guilt of the citizens to a sense of honor.

It was 1970. It's fair to say that back then a new state of war was brewing between the

US government and many Native Americans, from reservations to urban communities. It was not only a state of war where gunfire and violence were exchanged, but it was a state of war in the minds of many of us. Some Indians felt reborn in this state of war. Toward the end of the chant there is a reference to the Iroquois name for the Great Mystery. The intention of its use is to reach those Native people everywhere who have forgotten about the Mystery, and to beckon them to remember.

On that afternoon in the darkened den of my uncles' home, we drummed on the warrior's drum together, Uncle Nip and I, while I spoke into song the words of the chant. My beating began steady, almost slowly, my uncle's beating, though along with me, more powerful, and every now and then he would pound the beat on the drum with great force again and again and again . . . *Boom! Boom!*

As I beat a slow steady beating, I sang,

> *Comes the need of bright honor*
> *Comes the need . . .*

My uncle Nip, keeping beat with me, suddenly pounded once. *Boom!* The power jolted my heart.

> *From the sands of Gulf waters*
> *From the grove dappled shoreline*
> *Down the ridges of time, coming fast, coming faster*
> *Comes that need, comes that need now*

He pounded again, *Boom!* and then our beating together resumed.
> *From the land of my fathers*
> *Through the pines and the chestnuts*
> *Comes the need . . .*
> *Comes the urge on my song*

Down the slopes of Mount Rainier
Past its glaciers and meadows
Through its flowers at snow line
That need sings in my song

Up from Baja, past Salt Lake—He pounded again, Boom!
On the wide Mississippi
Down the winds of the Great Plains
Comes the need, comes my song

Drifting slow in the pollens of Sakoiatisan
Whispering wet in the rains gusting wide on the winds
Laughing bright as fall flowers in the mists of the morning
Comes the need . . .
Comes the need on my song

And all the while, to emphasize an emotion of power, a statement of power, he would continue to pound again and again and again.

On the dust of the thundering herds of the bison
Their gray, ghosted manes flowing free in the wind
On the fog drifting softly like spirits of dead leaves
In the sun pools and shadows warming, cooling the ghosts
Of my people all waiting, waiting now for my song
Comes the need of bright honor . . .
Comes the urge . . . comes the need,
comes the need now.

Up from sad Osamekun's old kindness, old largesse
Through the ant-eaten sockets of Metacom's skull

No ending to his pounding *Boom! Boom! Boom! Boom!* and my steady beating.

Past the memories of Sand Creek, ruins of Pueblo Bonito
Out of kivas and longhouses rotting in time
Comes the need . . . , the need and the urge
Comes the bright shining honor, comes its need
comes its urge

From the halls of Montezuma, from the shores of Tripoli

Pounding again, once, twice . . . *Boom! Boom!*

Oh beautiful for spacious skies
Can't you see, can't you see, oh say can't you see
What you've done to my people, my land, and to me?
Comes the urge, comes the need
Past your hate, past your greed
Through your minted and printed your coinaged lust
That I perjure myself with your "In God we trust"
As the Great Holy Mystery inhabits the dust
Of your glassed Constitution, your framed Bill of Rights
That proud Declaration and all the dark nights
You have rained on the world with bombs from the heights
You have scaled and the depths of delights

You have plumbed in your extirpative fights

My country 'tis of thy Pequot and Heuchi

The Beothuk, Cayuse, Calusa, Caloucha

Thy Inkpa, Ihasha, thy Ika, Henuti

Peoria, Secawgo, Carises, Cajueche

All, all the forgotten dead tribes and dead nations

You killed with your guns and your handkerchief rations

And smallpox-rich blankets, your Fort Pitt donations

Oh, my country 'tis of thy sermons, orations

that deny us God's grace shed on thee

Can't you see, can't you see, oh say can't can't you see

What you've done to my people, my land, and to me?

May your God and Sakoiatisan both let it be

That the need of bright honor may yet come to free

Us from you, from your justice, your freedom, and last

From our own dismal error: forgetting our past

In our present forgetting to still hear the word

Sakoiatisan sent us: Sakoiatisan heard.

Comes the need of bright honor . . .

Comes that need now from me.

The drumming did not cease at the end of the chant. The drumming continued. Faster. The chant continued. More melodic, but faster. More sung than spoken. And again we would begin the song without stopping and, again, it would be faster, stronger, again and again. This went on in that time that cannot be measured as we know it.

The room fell absolutely silent when it was over, but the vibration, now energy, of the drum and the song filled it. We were in the energy. We had poured the energy into the world. It was all around us. I would rest on the floor exhausted in this sacred moment with my back against the recliner; the drum, now silent, on the stand in front of me; my uncle on his knees near me, still and quiet, too.

A month or so later, he called me into his office at the university and showed me a copy of *Literature of the American Indian*. He opened it, and showed me the page where it read at the top, "A Chant to Lure Honor."

PART FIVE

THE FIRST SOUND

I have learned that before anything could be created, sound had to come forth. That sound from the Great Mystery has been called the word, and that word, my uncles would one day write, "is vital to the Great Mystery, being perhaps the greatest mystery, for it has the power to cause medicine to work, to lure animals into hunting range, to cause plants to grow, to allow man to address, be heard by, and join with the Great Mystery."

—EXCERPT FROM *LITERATURE OF THE AMERICAN INDIAN*

Before the Beginning of the New-Making, Awonawilona solely had being. Nothing else existed, save everywhere black darkness, and void desolation. Then Awonawilona conceived within the Mystery of its own being and thought outward into space . . .

—ADAPTED FROM A TRIBAL CREATION ACCOUNT

The most widely accepted theory for the origin of our universe is called the Big Bang theory. It theorizes that our universe evolved from a singularity—unimaginably dense, unimaginably hot, and unimaginably small. It was originally called the Big Bang because the scientists of the time construed the sudden expansion of the singularity as an explosion—"Where did it come from? We don't know. Why did it appear? We don't know."

—PARAPHRASED, IN PART, FROM *ALL ABOUT SCIENCE*

CHAPTER FIFTEEN

WE DO NOT HEAR, WE FEEL

What is the first sound that we do not hear, but we feel?

From the moment our process of gestation begins within the saltwater wombs of our mothers, we are vibration, vibration emanating from somewhere in the universe too distant for any human being to imagine, and yet, so close it occupies our very centers. Some call it soul. Some say spirit. It is that part of us that is all things. As we grow inside this womb, and our form begins to evolve around the spirit, another vibration draws our awareness, closer to what we are becoming. Perhaps, during the process of our transition from female to a determined sex, or from amphibian to human, we are conscious of the encompassing rhythm of not only the ever-present one now emanating from our mothers, but at some point in our gestation, we can hear the beating rhythm emanating from ourselves.

They say that the heart of the unborn and the heart of the mother can attain synchronicity, beating in time together. It is said that if this does not happen, even once during the gestation and birth, something may be wrong.

For those of us born without this experience, we may sense as we grow older an unidentifiable absence of something we cannot put into words. Long after our births, when we attune our heartbeat with another's, we may understand what we had been missing. If our hearts don't experience that synchronicity with another, we may unconsciously have the need to fill that absence we have yet to identify, unfortunately, with things that do not fulfill, or replenish, the spirit. Alcohol. Drugs. Overindulgence. Self-centeredness. Always wanting more . . . Lack of gratitude. Greed. The constant need for attention through negative behavior. Power over others. Violence. Killing for sport, killing beyond the need to survive.

Many of us feel lost in this world from time to time. Some of us can't even identify the origin of the feelings that bring us down.

Oftentimes, our infant lives begin severed from that original sound of drumming. That original vibration. It seems that we grow older only hearing our hearts' rapid and strong pulsations when our blood pressure is too low or too high, or as a result of strenuous physical activity, as well as heightened emotions. These quicken or slow the drumming of our hearts. But, generally speaking, our human bodies developing outside the womb now, even with artificial stimulation or slowing heartbeats, serve perhaps only as subconscious and distant reminders that we no longer attach to the origin of our beginnings, nor to the origin of all things.

And therein dwells an emptiness, a hollowness inside of us that we may never fill until the drum enters our ears and touches our hearts, until the pulse of life synchronizes with our own. Even for the instant that we do perceive the drum, the sound may be too incoherent for us to grasp it, and we may not know any better than to let it go.

. . . .

And yet, if we could recognize where this all went wrong, we may understand how we got this way, and what we need to do to get out of it. The medicine can be in your hands . . .

Begin the drumbeat as it comes to you. Say the words from the old song until saying the words becomes the singing that accompanies the beating of your heart, and the beating of the drum. Imagine it as an incantation for insight into the darker depths of your self, and assistance in emerging out . . .

> *My own mind is very hard to me.*
> *Way-hay, way-hay hee*
> *It is just as if I were carrying my mind around. Way-hay, way-hay hee*
> *What is the matter with you?*
> *What is the matter with me?*
> *Way-hay, way-hay hee*

Since the drum is often the only instrument used in our sacred rites, I should perhaps tell you here why it is especially sacred and important to us. It is because the round form of the drum represents the whole universe, and its steady strong beat is the pulse, the heart, throbbing at the center of the universe.

It is the voice of Wakan Tanka, and this sound stirs us and helps us to understand the Mystery and power of all things.

—BLACK ELK (LAKOTA)

CHAPTER SIXTEEN

THE SOUND WE NEED TO HEAR,
THE SOUND WE NEED TO MAKE

Once many of us hear the pounding of the drum, we can, at last, become affected in that special way. No matter at what age the introduction, the first time our heartbeat pounds in rhythm with the ancient beat of the drum, we will once again be fused with the heart of the Great Mother of all beings in the world, the Earth Mother, and reconnected in consciousness to the Original Source of All Things, the Great Holy Mystery.

They say that while we gestate in the womb, our hearts beat slowly in their rhythms. Then they can speed up, much like a dance that starts off with an unhurried drumbeat and gradually increases in speed, and we pick up our dancing to synchronize our steps and our heartbeats with the drum, the souls of our moccasins, or our sneakers, or our bare feet, the souls of our being in these human forms, dancing and singing the rhythms of life on the body of our sacred Mother. These moments transform the primal power of our sense of being into what Spirit truly feels like within this human experience.

During the gestation in the womb of our mothers, we sense vibration even before our ears develop. Then, at one point in the developmental process, we begin to hear beyond the womb—first our mother's voice, then sounds of various kinds, all affecting our own growth and the rhythms of our newly evolving hearts and the keenness of our senses. It would be so wonderful during these times to bring the unborn to natural places, places where the sounds of nature influence the life inside the womb. If not the pounding of waves near the shore and the rush of water onto the beach, then in a park where even the presence of squirrels and birds, and the sounds of wind moving through trees, have their influences.

And with one's own hand drum
With gentle beats and singing,
Such sacred influence
The growth of the unborn.
The drums of mother or father now beat in rhythm,
Becoming one with the pulse beating from the mother's heart,
even the father's,
And then the beat of the unborn
Inside the womb
Evolves
In a cosmic comfort happy
Of the continuing connection
Through the beating
To the origin of all births on this planet,
Mother Earth,
And to the origin of all origins,
the Great Holy Mystery.

THE TURNING OF TEALA

Holly Reese

Unlike all my previous pregnancies, this one was easy. No morning sickness, no cravings, no pain or fear or surprises. Once I removed the internal medical device keeping me from having any more children, Teala began her journey into this world immediately. I knew this child before she was conceived and she had broken my resistance.

Her godmother dreamed of Teala as well, lying on her back on a blanket of grass where the only light came from the millions of bright stars above her. The stars whirled and moved in a circular motion and became an immense web. Through this web, dolphins jumped and swam.

I was not surprised.

When I was heavy with Teala, I called him, the keeper of the grandfather drum, after a doctor's appointment and confided my worry about the diagnosis that the baby was breech, and they were talking to me about the possibility of a caesarian section. I was told she was too far along to turn. I did not want to bring this baby into the world with a surgery. All of my other children had been delivered naturally, and I was confused as to why this child refused to be upside down.

I went to the drumkeeper's house that evening and he brought out a ceremonial drum so large I had never seen anything like it.

It was the Grandfather Drum, which he called "medicine," and in the quiet night he began to awaken us all.

The drum is our heartbeat.

As he played, we fell, trancelike, away into our connection with our Mother, the Earth, and beyond to the Great Mystery and the universe . . .

This great drum beat all night. The powerful vibrations filled the small room, full of Indigenous art and the smell of sage, cedar, and sweetgrass. Every beat reached out and penetrated the flesh of my full belly, moving the water and caressing Teala, even as it moved through me. My entire being and spirit waxed and waned to the sound and feel of this tide. The ocean moves, waves consistently hitting the shore, again and again, unceasing throughout eternity.

I saw him, through closed eyes, reach out to caress her, and gently nudge on her back as she danced to the beat of her mother's heart and the drum, synchronizing to the sound of the universe.

And the baby turned.

It was painful, as she stretched and prepared to come into this life. When the drum ceased, dawn had broken and the small house was still full of the sound of the drum behind the sound of birds and the beginning of a new Florida day.

Teala came into the world, head down, several weeks later. A beautiful caramel Native child with dark hair and eyes and a clear white deer hoofprint on her back, behind her heart. Twenty-one now, she is a wild, Indigenous soul who loves Mother Earth, all creatures, and her family.

Life is filled with magic and mystery. Teala tells me that she conceived on the day I awakened this memory. She is now heavy with child herself. Her birthmark remains, a clear white hoofprint on her back. She wears it with pride and anxiously awaits this new child as the waves crash, insistently against the shore. Her child dances in her belly to the beat of her mother's heart, to the rhythm of the Mystery, to the insistence that our blood remains and that we remember.

—HOLLY REESE, SENIOR AND TRANSGENDER PROGRAMS MANAGER AT THE GAY AND LESBIAN COMMUNITY CENTER OF SOUTHERN NEVADA, CHOCKTAW NATION.

CHAPTER SEVENTEEN
WITH THE DRUM WE ARE INVINCIBLE

In the womb, what a wonderful time to be exposed to the sound of the drum, a father beating on a hand drum, a mother doing the same. Men's beating on the big drum at powwows and ceremonies of healing, of being born, and thanksgivings, and giveaways, and honoring. Even during heated protests for treaty rights and human rights and Earth rights. I have watched and been a part of protests where young pregnant women carried their unborn, committed to making the world a better place for their children. I have seen this. I have heard this. That pounding rhythm of the drums on the steps of a courthouse, beating for the right of Native women to be free of violence; even outside the iron gates and guard towers of a state penitentiary, and I have heard the drums, and seen the defiant men, and these women with their bellies swollen, supporting and beautiful, protecting life, exposing the goodness of this creative energy that is the life they carry, as the power of the songs on the drum the singers sing, forming a connection, a bond, to our tribal and primal origins, and to our Mother Earth in ways that nothing else can. I have felt that power. I have felt the energy stir when I heard the drums, swear as though we were invincible. And maybe, for an instant, with the pounding warrior drums and songs of the singers, the female energy, and new life energies, encircling us all, for that moment, we were . . .

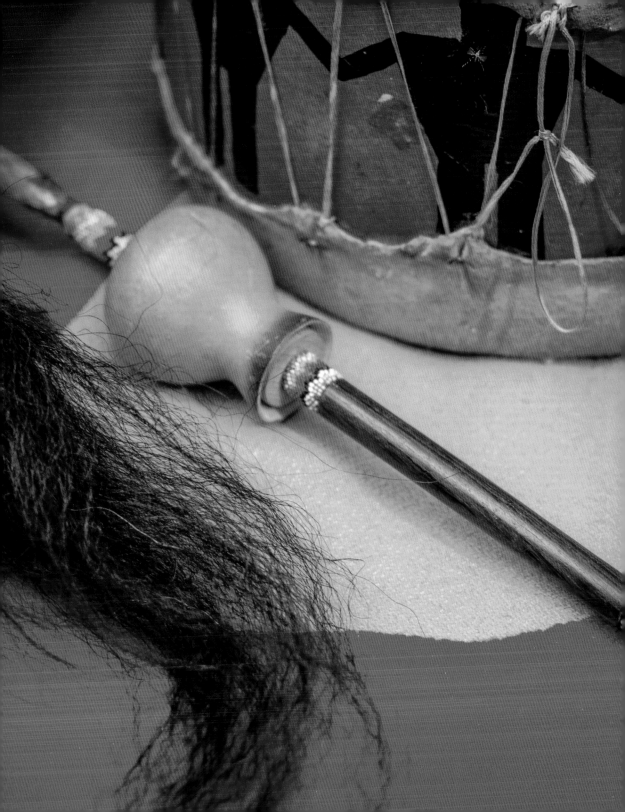

PART SIX

TOBACCO

It was many years ago. Maybe thirty, maybe forty . . .

My older Cherokee relative said to a young man who was talking with us with great passion about the new movement of Indians that was sweeping the country and how he felt that "the old people needed to get onboard"; and all the while he spoke, he smoked a cigarette.

"Why are you swearing?" the elder asked.

The young man appeared perplexed. Then he glanced down, as if instinctively he understood. The cigarette dangling from his fingers, ashes dropping to the ground—he became embarrassed.

The Origin Stories of Tobacco May Vary, But the Sacredness of Tobacco's Meaning Does Not

It has been said that, in ancient times, when the land was barren and the people were starving, Manitou sent forth a woman to save humanity. As she traveled over the world, everywhere her right hand touched the soil, there grew potatoes. And everywhere her left hand touched the soil, there grew corn. And when the world was rich and fertile, she sat down and rested. When she arose, there grew tobacco . . .

—FROM A TRIBAL ACCOUNT

CHAPTER EIGHTEEN

THE TEACHING OF OCKABE'WIS, THE MESSENGER

It has been said, "The people on the First Earth were not wise." They did not know about clothing. They did not know about shelter. They did not know how to make a fire. "Then the spirit of the one who creates sent a man to teach them. This man was called Ockabe'wis [Messenger]." When he asked them why they were sitting around doing nothing, they replied, "Because we do not know what to do."

They say that these first people "did not use their minds." They had "no ideas of their own, only to do what Ockabe'wis told them to do." This was on the First Earth, "long before Winabojo." Many Indigenous peoples understand through tribal literature that there have been four worlds prior to this one. Not necessarily meaning from otherworldly planets, but perhaps different worlds right here on Earth. Different stages, considering the Earth is over four billion years old. Science supports this concept. Some tribes and nations say that this is the Fourth World. Others say the Fifth. But, one thing is for certain: They agree that there were previous stages of existence.

And so, on this First Earth, time passed, and they say, Ockabe'wis taught the first people many things: how to make clothes; how to make shelter; how to make fire of decayed wood. But, in order to teach them how to use their minds . . . "Ockabe'wis told them that they must fast and find out things by dreams and that if they paid attention to these dreams they would learn how to heal the sick."

Now it has been said of this time very long ago, "The people [of the First Earth] listened and fasted and found in dreams and visions how to teach their children and do everything. The young men were taught that they must regulate their lives by dreams;

they must live moral lives, be industrious, and be moderate in the use of tobacco when it should be given to them. They were especially taught that their minds would not be clear if they ate and drank too much. Tobacco and corn were given to them, but it was Ockabe'wis [the messenger] who taught them how to use them."

—ADAPTED FROM *LITERATURE OF THE AMERICAN INDIAN*

Once, a First Nations grandmother from Canada handed me tobacco leaves from a plant that genetically went back a thousand years. The Indigenous people where she lived had cared for this plant, and their ancestors had cared for this plant, through many generations because the plant is sacred. Nearby on a reservation within the borders of the United States, there was a twenty-first-century conflict among these same tribal people about whether to sell tobacco on their reservation. In this way, American citizens can buy cigarettes without the high state taxes. An attractive purchase and discount, especially if one is addicted to cigarette smoking, for cigarettes are designed with chemicals for that very purpose.

The conflict over whether to sell tobacco on the reservation became violent at times. The power of money and its contemporary influences cannot be exaggerated. Of course, the argument in favor of tobacco sales was that the profits from the sale of tobacco would benefit their impoverished tribe. The traditionalists asserted that selling tobacco for uses beyond what it was originally intended for was paramount to giving up one's Indigenous soul—a kind of "selling" of one's culture.

Tobacco is used for medicine. Tobacco is used as an offering to our ancestors in prayer, the traditional people asserted.

If we do this, no good can come from such a thing. Tobacco is used during our most sacred ceremonies. Tobacco is used in our sacred pipes. Tobacco is used as an offering to the drums that we keep and care for. Maybe to feed our children we can exchange tobacco for food and shelter and such. But what if we understood that the tobacco we sold was to be used by a civilized people who have no sacred regard for the plant? Who purposefully adds chemicals to our sacred plant, specifically to addict anyone who smokes? Would that be right? Can we still call ourselves Indians and do this?

Even Indigenous people can become victims of this addiction, which was why the teachings were specific to the plant's use. I was taught that "medicine has two sides." Clearly, being Indigenous in the civilized world has its complications.

And though I have seen new buildings, and even new schools built on some of the reservations that were paid for, in part, by the sale of tobacco, I have also seen too many grab the check and run, and fat cat politicians, tribal and otherwise, who have their own pockets filled. And I have seen and heard of the material wealth and waste that result from the sale of tobacco.

And then what becomes of the sacred plant the messenger had taught us how to use? the old ones ask. *What becomes of us? How much power can our tobacco offerings have if we abuse the very plant that turns our prayers into smoke, that lifts our prayers to the Sky, that vibrates on the drum upon whose skin we beat and sing?*

Such abuse, they say, *would be tantamount to swearing and lying and using words to manipulate others for our own gain. If we use language in this way, how can we use language then to pray, or sing our songs on the drum, and expect our words to have power any longer?*

ALL MY RELATIONS

Within my hand I hold my brother, father,

Grandfather, sister, mother, and grandmother.

Within my hand I hold the true spirit of giving.

Within my hand I hold knowledge of past and future.

Within my hand I hold the selflessness of sacrifice.

Within my hand I hold the hopes and prayers of life.

Within my hand I hold all my relations.

Within my hand is tobacco.

—MARK SELF, INDIGENOUS POET, SINGER, AND DRUMMER,
1975 GRADUATE OF HEART OF THE EARTH SURVIVAL SCHOOL.

PART SEVEN

THE PRACTICE OF CONSCIOUS THOUGHT

. . . don't forget natural time, even though we must live in a world that is also run by the clocks of man-made time . . . To forget the passage and cycles of natural time would also be to forget your kinship with the Earth, the Sun, the Moon, and the Stars. And that would be awful . . . For nothing can make us feel so empty than separation from our kin.

—FROM *MOTHERLESS*

To us this is beautiful and fitting, symbol and reality at the same time, expressing the harmony of life and nature. Our circle is timeless, flowing; it is new life emerging from death—life winning out over death.

—JOHN (FIRE) LAME DEER (LAKOTA)

Everything I imagine our ancestors did was a reflection of what they saw in nature. They were students of nature, from conscious awareness after birth, until separation at death. The symbols on their homes, their clothes, on their instruments of war and prayer, and those they fastened to the pipes and rattles and their drums, all had meaning. The colors had meaning. The understanding was that the energy (the vibration) of those symbols would be drawn to the energy of the objects, and our people would use this energy to make things happen. Sometimes, actions, as well, can be symbolic and transcend the act itself . . .

CHAPTER NINETEEN

SUNWISE

Because many drums are created in circles, we are often reminded when we see them of the great circle of life of which we all share a part. I used to tell classroom teachers of Native children when I got the chance to speak with them, "There are no front rows or back rows in a circle. Everyone has an equal place in the circle. In the circle we see each other's faces, not the backs of our heads."

They say, *Nature wants things to be round. The trunks of trees. The trunks of elephants. A turtle's eggs. The forms of our bodies. The roundness of the Earth, our Mother. The Sun. The Moon.*

They say, *The way the Sun travels the Sky . . . The way the Moon circles the Earth . . . The way the Earth turns on her axis . . . The way the planets orbit the Sun . . . The way the Sun moves through the galaxy . . . All round and moving in circles and we moving together with them . . . on our way with the galaxy spiraling toward the Black Hole at the center . . .*

Everything moves in circles and cycles, it seems. Looking down at the warrior drum, I am reminded of the wholeness . . . the Oneness . . . the Totality. And so, to mimic the powers of Creation, when we gather in especially sacred moments, we form a circle. However, I have sat at a square table sipping coffee and talking with young people and elders about issues of the people, and spiritual meanings within the mysteries of life, and even at that square table, where we may have been joking and playing cards, we had formed a circle. A circle is a way of perception. Some of our drums are different shapes for different reasons, but still the circle is there because it is a way of perception—each beat a circle rippling through the world and the universe.

I learned to enter a purification lodge going to my left, *Sunwise*.

I learned to pass a sacred pipe going to the left, *Sunwise*.

Clockwise, this passing to the left, or sunwise, I had been taught as a young man, and had observed over the years, mimics the flow of creation. In this way we help establish synchronicity, and harmony, with the movement of the world and the cosmos that we share. When we do this with conscious thought, our relationship with creation grows stronger, becomes more intimate and influential.

They say that *if we want to evoke the powers of the Thunder Beings, then pass things to the right; for we know how a hurricane turns, we know how a tornado whirls, we know the wind's greatest power is that movement. It can be destructive . . . Even when I was a teacher passing out papers for my class, I always started to my left.*

CHAPTER TWENTY

A NAMING CEREMONY WITH THE PIPE AND THE DRUM

It was sometime in the early to mid-seventies; I was on a reservation that borders North and South Dakota. It was a time when tribal police and officials, along with local law enforcement and the FBI, were known to have broken into Indigenous people's homes and destroyed their sacred things, their holy objects. They broke necklaces and rattles and smashed drums. They defiled pipes and medicine bags. They often prohibited traditional ceremonies or disrupted them, even making arrests when people protested. After all, it wasn't until 1978 that the Indigenous people in the United States were allowed to practice traditional spiritual expression with the passage of the American Indian Religious Freedom Act.

(Kind of puts things into perspective.)

The tribal government had warned that anyone from AIM would be arrested if they came onto the reservation. *We don't need any outside agitators. There will be no ceremony.* Well, I was an AIM survival school teacher, so that associated me with AIM. AIM was considered "armed and dangerous." I have never owned a gun, though I have always kept my bow where I can find it.

I was also living in Minneapolis, so I would be considered an outside agitator, a label used on me before, and others as well, and would be again. Still, I swear, the green Gremlin we were riding in that day through the Dakotas might have been invisible when we entered reservation territory. We were never stopped, coming, or going . . .

The ceremony involved a long walk up a winding trail that led over and through the hills of the northeastern Dakotas. When we reached a clearing on the plateau of one hill, we formed a wide circle where over a hundred people of all ages—men, women, and children—found their places in the sacred directions, and sat on the Earth. To protect and respect individual privacy, I will leave a few things out, but the story essentially happened in this way.

In the north direction of the circle, a few elders sat on the ground on old chairs, around a big drum. In the center of the great circle of people was the boy who would be named, a name his great-great grandfather, who had been severely wounded in World War I, was passing down to him, taking on another name for himself.

The old warrior could not make the journey up the hills, but I saw him before we left the house, sitting back in his chair, his arms on the arms of the chair, his knees higher than the arms of the chair. "You know," he said, after just meeting me. I sat down in another chair. "You know," he repeated, "got shot up pretty bad in the First World War. Needed a complete blood transfusion . . . If it hadn't been for some generous white man giving me blood, I would've died. So, when I wanted to run for tribal office, they had a blood quota question on the application form: What percent Indian blood? I wrote on that paper, I ain't got a drop of Indian blood in me." And then he laughed. "But I still ran for tribal council."

I imagined him, as I unwrapped the Great Mystery pipe on the hill as I imagine him even now, sitting back in his chair, watching the ceremony with his eyes closed and his back to the window, his hand tapping the arm of the chair in rhythm with the drum a mile or so away . . .

I peer into the mist of memory, recalling the brightness of the day itself, the scent of the sweetgrass smoke bathing each sacred object, and the people themselves, as I stood standing with the boy and his grandmother in the center of the grand circle as the pipe was filled with tobacco, and we introduced him to the universe. To see, and feel, the power of this elderly woman as she lifted the pipe into the air and spoke the new name of her grandson was so strong it could have lifted us off the hill. She held the sacred pipe up to the four directions, Sky and Earth, and to Wakan Tanka, and spoke the young man's name.

Then, once again, as would happen in a Minnesota prison a few years later, I picked up a hand drum and sang . . . *All is Sacred/All is Beautiful,* and I chanted softly with the drumbeat to help lift the prayers to the Mystery, into the Oneness of All Things. As the pipe was passed hand to hand, and each person, young and old, male and female, said words of prayer and smoked that day in the circle in the high hills of Indigenous country, the Sun shined in a cloudless Sky, and the wind swept gentle breezes to keep us cool, and the pipe never went out. It is also important to note that there have been times at such gatherings when the numbers of the people suddenly, or gradually, have multiplied, and would increase to even double the number sometimes when we started—something that disturbed the American settlers and military less than eighty-five years earlier, when the drumming and songs of the Ghost Dance Movement ended in the massacre and bloody snow at Wounded Knee. No one on the hill, conscious of them that day for the naming, doubted that these were the ghosts of the land. These were the ancestors, participating in the mysterious ways they can.

After the pipe completed its journey, the older men began to sing and beat on the big warrior's drum. I thought to myself, *These were the men responsible during the most difficult times of keeping sacred things alive, to have kept the songs alive, and the drum secure.* When the churches and government officials were running helter-skelter all over Indian country, attempting to dismantle whatever it was that made Indians Indians, these were the ones who avoided the human plague of cultural genocide, for they had concealed the drums, and remembered the songs.

The churches still do this unapologetically today, sometimes with a bit more subtlety, committing cultural genocide right before our eyes and doing so in the name of education or to help impoverished people. Something like what Sea World has been doing to orcas, stealing their spirit, exploiting their beauty, under the guise of education. Of course, this is from my Indigenous perspective. Hell, the way I see it, they're doing it right now in the public schools. The churches, though, may be the worst, only they are a little trickier about it.

The day of naming on that hill, in the presence of a sacred pipe, there was no American flag. There was no singing of the national anthem. There was the great circle of the people. There were the yellow, red, black, and white flags of the four directions. There were beautiful ribbon dresses and handsome shirts and impeccable beadwork, and a colorful star quilt the women had made.

The older men drummed on a big drum, and sang the old songs, and behold! Above us, soared two eagles. Everyone's eyes fixed on these magnificent birds as they ascended and circled above us. It was a most holy sight in a most sacred place. They circled the whole time the men sang on the drum. They circled right up into the Sky, taking the songs of the men on the drum, the energies of all our love, and a young man's new name with them . . .

SIXTEEN EAGLES
John Leith

As a child growing up in this world, the drum was the heartbeat of my soul. It made my life feel good to hear the singers and dancers behind the drum. The drum is the circle of our life. If you look around, everything is the circle of life. When I was young, I was at a powwow in Wisconsin. They were singing at the drum; we all looked up. There were sixteen eagles circling the powwow as they sang. When the singers were done, the eagles flew away.

—JOHN LEITH, MUSICIAN, 1976 GRADUATE OF THE RED SCHOOL HOUSE.

CHAPTER TWENTY-ONE

PERCEPTIONS OF POWER: MALE AND FEMALE ENERGY AND THE DRUM

When my uncles told me they were getting too old to care for the grandfather warrior drum, they said that it was time for me to carry on the responsibility.

Though for an instant collapsing at such responsibility within the idea, I took a deep breath. "Of course, uncles," I replied, and felt the passing of time and generations as I never had before.

"We are proud of you, Gabriel. We are proud of our nephew. We know the drum will be in good hands. You sang your chant on this drum. Songs of power and medicine have been sung to the beat of this drum. Women have stood around this drum and lent their voices to the men and to the beating of the drum's heart. For the heartbeat of this drum is for them, too. But, first, you must understand, a girl or a woman should not touch this drum. Never. This was the teaching passed on to us. On this drum, songs of death and war to defend our people and our country have been sung. They may need to be heard again. A woman's innate power has been to nurture, not destroy life. Her power has been to give life, nourish creativity, should she decide to do so, not to kill, not to destroy, although these would be her choices as well. Still, with this drum, we must honor what has been passed down.

I understood what they were telling me. No one respected women of the old ways more than my uncles. They respected all people who had earned that respect. But I also understood the responsibility passed on to me. I would hear, and read the words of elders many years later, that at certain times, a woman's energy, and the energy of certain sacred objects or ceremonies, would clash in power like hot air rising from the South meeting cold air descending from the North. Neither is greater than the other. That is the way of nature. It's real and must be respected. The elders would say that they did not want to be responsible for causing harm as a result of that clash of power. I also understand that women have been mistreated and treated unfairly in this country and in the world. But this is not about that. This is about respecting power. This is about the warriors who would give their lives in defense of the women and children.

This idea of a girl or woman not touching the warrior's drum was not something that was thought up to practice suppression of female energy, nor to demean in any way the power of women. It was to protect a woman's power and to protect the power of the warrior's drum. It was to respect the teachings passed down through time because they made sense to us.

THE RED SCHOOL DRUM, LED BY THE LATE PORKY WHITE

My uncles had taught me that male and female were equal beings. Father Sky/Mother Earth. In many of the American Indigenous tribes and nations, women were held in high regard. Among the Iroquois, it was the women who chose the male leadership, and it was the women who could take it away should a man prove incapable. Earth and Sky are equal, I would be told: Different beings, different roles, but equal. For many of us, women were our clan mothers, and it is true that they were leaders from time to time; they were warriors from time to time as well, men following them into battle.

My uncles told me that Princess Red Wing, aware of the warrior's drum presentation to me, would not want to leave my daughter Calusa out, since my two sons could beat on the warrior's drum. Red Wing discussed the idea of passing a drum on to Calusa. This one drum she had in mind was the one she most often traveled with when she was an invited speaker. Oftentimes, she would begin her presentation by four beats to each of the four directions, clearing the path for her words to follow, clearing the path for the goodness that would return. As she beat on her drum, she would address each direction, acknowledging their uniqueness and power, whether this was before an elementary school class or at a forum at a major university. This was the drum she would pass on to my daughter, even though Calusa was still a small child. My uncles and Red Wing explained to her that women have been the ones to beat on Red Wing's drum. They said that if Calusa chose, she could allow her brothers that privilege, but only if she gave them permission. And, of course, they looked at her brothers when they told her this.

Now, this idea may not sit well with some women today who rightfully insist that male and female are equal. But, "equal" does not mean the same. Powers can be unique to each. Back in the '60s and '70s, when I was more active in tribal ceremonies and pow-wows and such, I never recall seeing women beating on a big powwow drum. I assumed they didn't because of what I had been taught about the warrior's drum. I never saw women and men together beating on a big drum. What I saw was the men singing and beating, and the women encircling the men, standing behind them and around them, lending their voices of female power to the song. The symbolism was powerful!

I was taught that among some tribes, the men cleared the fields for the garden because clearing the fields meant trees may have to be cut, plants removed at the roots. There had to be killing. After the men had cleared the land, they planted the seeds.

But after that, it was the women who cared for the garden. The women nurtured the growth of the garden. They sang to their gardens as they worked, and to the babies of the next generation as they swayed in cradle boards from the branches of nearby trees. This was how it was told to me . . .

Among certain Indigenous peoples, men were not even allowed in the garden at this time because of their energy. The male energy that must kill to survive and sometimes to defend the community might clash with the female power of the women and the garden. Only when the crops were ready for harvest, I was taught, would the men be allowed to participate, though words and phrases in English like "not allowed" to do this and "allowed" to do that, when spoken, cannot convey the idea of the meaning, nor the understanding. That can only come from teaching and observing nature, and observing the behaviors of grown-ups.

In these days there are women's drum groups, and on some tribal drums both women and men beat and sing. In a world as diverse as our own, there are always exceptions. There are always reasons. And, as such, always an opportunity for me to understand.

Everything is done with meaning and intent—every aspect of the drum, from the wood to the hide that covers the wood; to the kinds of feathers that are used; every color, every symbol. This is akin to a sacred pipe: Everything on the pipe has a power it draws when it is used for prayer and spiritual matters, and even to protect. It is the same with the drum. What we put on the drum comes from something special. On the warrior's drum in my keeping there are water moccasin medicine bags. The objects then draw certain energies to the drum that we want to come, or we may put something on the drum to protect the drum. We may have a special experience with something in nature, or something that came to us in a dream. Something that came to us out of love and respect for something we see in nature and feel especially close to. These are sacred things. In a way, it is not much different than when we wear a certain necklace or ring, or article of clothing, to keep close to us the love of a certain person. We apply total consciousness and coherency when they are in our keeping and when we use these things to decorate the drum.

CHAPTER TWENTY-TWO

SYMBOLISM AND ITS POWER

I can't imagine painting a symbol on my drum if I didn't understand what it meant.

Is it something I dreamed?

Is it something that happened to me, something that enlightened me, shared power with me?

I can't understand why I would use a symbol of an animal, a star, a plant, or a tree, an insect or a fish, if I didn't know what it meant to me. The power it draws to me and the drum.

A dolphin or a whale. A salmon or a snow crab. What do they symbolize?

What power am I seeking to help me with my beating?

Colors: Red, black, white, and yellow usually represent the four sacred directions.

In what direction is each placed and what is its meaning? Blue is sometimes used. And Green, too. Everything. Every design. Every feather. Even what I wear around my neck has meaning, symbolism, power . . .

They decorate our sacred things, our bodies, too.

We see them on the rocks on cliffs. Each petroglyph has meaning.

Each tells a story . . .

THE WINTER SPIDER DRUM OF PEACE

William Commanda (as told to Evan Pritchard)

One January morning, fifty or so years ago, an insect inspired Grandfather William Commanda, ninety-seven-year-old grand chief, wampum holder, and wisdom elder of the Anishinabe people, to make a special drum. He has never needed another.

This writing is based on a story he told me during a filmed interview, which was included in the unreleased film called *Makwah!* It is one of the best drum stories I ever heard.

So I had a back door to my wood shop. One morning, during the darkest days of winter, I unlocked the door and opened it. The cold air came blowing in and made me shiver. I went to pull a piece of dry wood out of the woodpile to make a fire inside the fireplace, inside the shop. There was this big spider standing there looking at me, as big as my fist, with a hundred legs or so, all around. Very black, inky-black like, black pipestone. What a big thing; I had never seen one that big!

I made a fire. After the fire got going, I put some hardwood into the fireplace to keep it burning. Then I came outside and I looked for that spider. I pulled here, pulled there. I had to rearrange all the boxes looking for that spider. It was thirty-five below zero. And I started to think, *How come that thing is still living out there in the open, and not frozen? That's not right, something is wrong.*

I went in the house, had my breakfast, and then went back out to search again for the spider. I didn't find it. I made another fire.

I started to bend some birch branches as if to make snowshoes. I bent it around to make a drum. It was about two feet across. It was sometime in January, the hardest, coldest time of the year, especially in the morning. That's when I found him, and that's where I put him, right in the center of my drum. I painted that giant black spider with many short black legs and two white eyes looking outward to the side.

He is sitting on a white surface of snow, surrounded by a sunburst of concentric zig-zag lines, a black line, a gold line, and a white line. The spikes of the sunburst touch the outer rim of the drum head. Between those spikes are triangles of red paint to complete the sunburst, representing the power of the spider, to bring about peace and to build the web of life. I placed that "spider"—its power for peacemaking—in my drum.

The outer surface of the frame is covered with red trade cloth, which generally represents the honoring of Mother Earth, according to tradition. I bent the wood into a circle using steam and heat. I use it to accompany myself when I sing the old songs. I don't have a voice anymore. My ninety-seven-year-old voice is not there anymore, but I do the best I can. When I used to sing in the church, the brothers had taught me to read notes, on four lines. I could sing anything in their book, just open it anywhere. The pianist would hit two notes on the piano, and I'd start singing. He'd start following me and we'd sing everything on the page.

Here is a heartbeat or round dance style of drumming (which includes the snake dance . . .)

Ay ay ya hey ya ho

Ay ay ya hey ya hey ya ho

Ay ay ya hey ya ho ay ya hey ya ho

Ay ay ya hey ya ho.

That's an old Indian song, one of my uncles taught me, my uncle's uncle, in fact. He came in drunk one time and started singing that song. It's a round dance. Sometimes they do a snake dance with this kind of song.

In order to make that drum to honor the spider, I had to find some deerskin, and quickly. My wife Mary, who has passed on now, had one deerskin. She had scraped it but had not smoked it yet. I stole it from her, and put it in my drum.

When she came to look for the deerskin to make something with it, she said, "Where's my skin?"

I said, "I don't know." She didn't recognize her skin stretched onto my drum! The one I had stolen from her! I placed a ring of wood in the center to tie all the strings together to give it strength. It's ash wood, the same type of wood I used for the frame, but this one is thinner, to bend it so that it is round, to make it strong.

I bent it with just my hands. In those days you didn't have any other choice. In the old days, my elders would never sing songs in the winter, as the notes would get frozen in the Sky somewhere. However, I still remember several snowshoe songs, which are sung while setting traplines in winter.

—WILLIAM COMMANDA, WHO PASSED AWAY AUGUST 3, 2011,
WAS BELOVED BY THE PEOPLE AS AN ALGONQUIN ELDER AND WISDOMKEEPER.
HE WAS ALSO KEEPER OF THE WAMPUM.

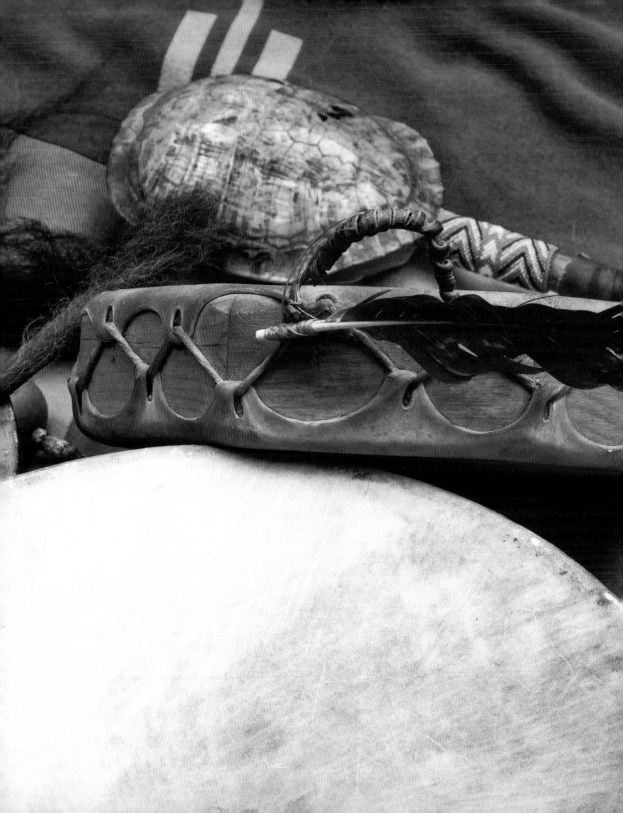

PART EIGHT

DRUM TEACHINGS

Words are the vibrations of nature. Therefore, beautiful words create beautiful nature.
Ugly words create ugly nature. This is the root of the universe.
—DR. MASARU EMOTO, *THE HIDDEN MESSAGES IN WATER*

In all that we do, exists the power of words . . .
—AMY KROUT-HORN

CHAPTER TWENTY-THREE

FIRST DRUM TEACHING: CHANGE LANGUAGE, CHANGE PERCEPTION

My, what have we done!

When I say, this is *my* land, I do not mean I own the land, in the denoted meaning of the possessive pronoun *my*. This is the land on which I live and the land I care for and the land that sustains me. Some of my family members are buried here. The land is Earth, and Earth is my Mother. I cannot own life, and Earth is life. English is a difficult language to use when expressing Indigenous philosophy. It is the same if we say this is "*my* drum" while speaking or writing. *I carried* my drum *to the water. I sang on* my drum. *I prayed on* my pipe. Using English we must be conscious of the words we choose so that we are understood, but we are not objectifying the drum or the pipe, or the land where we live, to imply ownership.

When Indigenous people speak of the theft of their land, the Indigenous intent is addressing an occupied territory. But again, territory and boundaries are not something that define ownership. Other humans who invade our territory often see land as a possession, as something you can own. They see life as an object to be acquired, rather than a fellow life form. Or if they do recognize life in animal or human form, they view it as a lower form of life because the invaders see themselves as superior to all other life forms. They justify their actions in their own minds, including the trickery used to acquire rights to another people's land, as well as the killing and stealing, if the legal and religious trickery does not work.

The military of the Americas, from Canada, through the United States, through Mexico, and into Central and South America, marched to their own drums with rifles and cannons on their way to participate in the slaughter. In South America today, it is not uncommon for men, operating the monstrous mechanical tree-killing earthmovers, to destroy the rain forest, while Latin music plays in their headphones as they rape the Earth.

To rational, thinking people, such acts of violence would be crimes against humanity. Crimes against nature. Tantamount to murder. It would be stealing. Are there religions in the world whose tenets sanction such behavior? You know the answer to that question. Are their special drums for marching soldiers who practice such behavior? You know the answer to that question as well. The land includes all the Indigenous life she has given birth to and sustains. Defending that land means defense of all those who share this philosophy. But I cannot *own* the land, never in an Indigenous perspective, no more than the birds own the trees or the dolphins own the ocean.

And so, if I need a piece of paper from a legal institution stating that this is my land, my property, I can obtain that, even though it has no spiritual value or meaning to me, and it makes no sense to me. But I live in a civilized world in which it does, so I compromise without sacrificing my integrity. And we adapt, and through our adaptation, we can survive.

Even *my* dog is not *mine. My* horse is not *mine. My* cat is not *mine.* This is my garden, but not in the denoted meaning. It is the garden of beautiful flowers I helped to create, and the garden I care for. Still, whenever I use the word *my,* how does the person hearing me interpret the connotation, and if I say *my* enough times, do I not then indoctrinate myself through its use until I assume that life really is *my* possession? *I own it.*

My wife, my life companion, is not *mine,* yet I have introduced her as *my* wife. I do not *own* her. She is not *my* possession. She is my companion and partner, who chooses to walk alongside me on this life journey. *My* children are not *mine,* either; yes, I am their human father, and when they were young, I had to be responsible for their sustenance and education, and their lives. I had to show them love. But they are the children of Earth and Sky.

Got to watch out for that word *my.*

Sure, we use it in casual conversation, and in writing, but we cannot fall into the trap it implies. *My* this; *my* that; mine . . . mine . . . mine. Again, say *my* and *mine* enough times and we begin to assume the meaning. And so, if we use these possessive pronouns, may we use them sparingly.

The drums in my care do not belong to me. I am the caretaker and keeper of these drums. The drums are living beings. Some are regarded as male drums, some female drums, some with both qualities, some with neither, simply forms of life. Because of their very existence in this world, they are vibration. It's quantum physics. I learned early on walking this path of heart, that I cannot own a pipe. I cannot own a drum. I have heard them called, along with other things we hold dear to us, sacred objects. Using the English language, this is one way to remind us of their specialness in our care. The word *sacred* provides this guidance.

But, again, we must be mindful of our language and our objectification of life. It is not romanticized to say that Indigenous people saw, and still see, rocks as living things. Mountains as alive. Water as alive. Each with spirit. I was taught that the closest I would get to owning anything would be my ownership of my physical body. So here's a prescriptive exercise to put into practice, now, before you pick up a drum again. Change the way you use the English language to better express an Indigenous perception: Be more aware of what you are saying with that language; challenge your intelligence; change perspective.

EVERYTHING IS VIBRATION

Everything is vibration. Everything in nature can therefore be considered alive.
The drum that we care for is not our property.
We cannot own vibration!
And so, the drum cannot belong in the sense of ownership to anyone.
A tribe may have drums for their needs, and a man or woman may have drums for personal use; each kept with honor and respect for life, and expressing the human condition . . .
For in the old way of thinking, it's a lot about the path we choose to walk and how we prepare our bodies and minds to walk that path, so we don't get too lost.
We cannot own something that is life.
We can, at most . . . provide protection, appreciation, love and cherish the drums in our care, that enable us to be drawn to a sacred rhythm
To keep in our trust.

CHAPTER TWENTY-FOUR

SECOND DRUM TEACHING: THE REVELATION OF THE SMALLEST WORD WITH THE GREATEST EFFECT

Here is one definition of the word *it*: "a direct object of a preposition, usually in reference to a lifeless thing . . . a plant, a person, or an animal whose sex is unknown . . . or disregarded . . ."

Key words here: *lifeless* and *disregarded*.

From childhood, we learn about life through language. We learn how to perceive the world and the universe through language, and we learn how to express our thoughts through language. As such, we become indoctrinated through language as well.

And so, as this indoctrination was passed on to us through language, we, in turn, indoctrinate our children. The consistent and frequent usage of such a word as *it* when referencing life gradually begins to indicate the absence of Indigenous intelligence, as well as feeling, when perceiving life, as life exists in the world, and in the universe . . .

No word could more openly, or subliminally, portray such a vast distinction between civilized thought and primal/Indigenous thought.

As a student of literature and writing and traditional Indigenous concepts, I was taught that English is a language of technology. Many Indigenous writers have always found it a challenge to translate Native thought into English for reasons such as this, and some things just can't be translated. This indicates what is lost when an Indigenous language is no longer spoken—which is why the churches and governments forbade them.

I learned that English is a male gender–biased language . . . In my childhood, I was taught that the First Cause of All That Is . . . is a male anthropomorphic being.

The rule of standard English further reinforces the human male dominion over the Earth and gender and species, and the male religious dominance over all the world through language.

As a writer of Indigenous philosophy, I must stay alert when it comes to word choice, definitions and usages, synonyms and such, and be aware of the context in which I use them.

I have heard elders who speak English as a second language, and elders who speak English as their primary language, use the word *it* when referencing another life form. I am not exempt from this. And, of course, we cannot assume that every life form in the Great Mystery has a specific gender. I mean, look at the diversity right here on Earth. We're talking about unlimited possibilities! This is another reason I was taught that Indigenous people did not attempt to define the Great Mystery. Definitions present limitations.

And, if we do refer to an object as an *it*, then we are probably referring to something inanimate, like a pencil, a car tire, a comma in a sentence, the trash that needs to be taken out or recycled. We can agree to use *it* in reference to these things. A rock is vibration, too. But I feel the rock is alive. I've participated in purification ceremonies when the glowing rocks placed into the center pit were welcomed as "grandfathers," a designation of respect, often translated from a Native language. Paying such close attention to the language we speak is hard, but the teaching remains: Language is sacred. For the language (choice of words) that we speak, regardless of the language we are speaking, reveals our perception of life and the world and the universe.

A drum may be a drum, but the term used to address the drum would be *grandfather*, or *grandmother* for some. Or, no gender assigned. But if you pick up the drum and say, "I'll sit with it over here," you are implying that the drum you brought to communicate and express your deepest and most sincere feelings, whether joyful, or playful, or sad, is not a living entity. Not a living being.

Do you see how the words we choose reflect how we see the world? If we say certain words, like *it*, enough times, without regard for the power of *its* connotative implications, when we reference a life form, especially when talking with children, the word *it* can eventually desensitize us and our children. And that's its purpose. That's its intent.

And so, as a teacher and a writer, I have labored over ways to describe or simply refer to living beings, avoiding the word *it* whenever I can. From the smallest of creatures to the biggest . . .

AN INDIGENOUS WORLDVIEW: IT IS NOT LIFE . . .

From a blade of grass to a tree to a forest . . . From an ant to an antelope; from a blue jay to an eagle . . .

From the Earth to the Sun, to the Moon, and planets and millions of other suns and stars . . .

To the universe and the Great Holy Mystery. And the drum we care for . . .

Life should never be objectified.

Say the word *it* enough times without thinking, without using our intelligence, and we assume the intention of the meaning. And that's an indoctrination process of separating ourselves from Nature.

And the world becomes an object for our use.

And the universe is filled with countless more objects.

Scientists rely on this, whether using animals for testing, exploring the resources here on Earth, or probing those on other worlds.

Militaries of industrialized nations, and corporations drilling for oil and shale, raping and fracking and gouging for diamonds, and mining deep inside our mountains for coal . . . uranium in the Earth's crust . . . Killing animals for sport and caging them for entertainment . . . Toxifying rivers and oceans and the Sky!

We have objectified them all with *it*!

But *it* is not a word in an Indigenous American language.

The drum in your hands, the drum we sit around and beat with our sticks and sing, the drums in our keeping must remain in our perceptions as all things that we see as life.

CHAPTER TWENTY-FIVE

THIRD DRUM TEACHING: YOUR SACRED PLACE AND TURTLE DRUM

You and your friend stand in your home, your friend admiring the special table where you've created a sacred space by the window. The sinking sunlight penetrates and warms the area. Come night, your friend will not be there when the moonlight casts a luminescent glow on the sacred space where you keep the sacred stones and crystals, the pretty shells, your incense and candles, maybe a braid of sweetgrass, and shavings of cedar, and a small bundle of sage, or even the resin rock of Mayan copal. And there in the center of your sacred space, a small clay bowl holds the pinches of your tobacco offerings to the painted turtle hand drum. Just beneath the support stand that holds the drum, lies the deerskin padded hickory stick you use to make the sacred sound.

Your friend sighs. "What a beautiful space!" But your friend's eye is drawn to the center of the table, to the drum. "Do you use it?" your friend asks.

You smile, and nod, your mind tripping back to the dawn of the day. You were sitting at the edge of your bed, beating a soft rhythm, a strong and gentle heart rhythm, and you were chanting as you faced the window with your eyes closed, seeing beyond the window, deeper into yourself. Some of the chanting consisted of words and some expressive sounds and incantations of your emotions. You can still feel the beat of the turtle drum in your heart; you've felt it upon occasion throughout the day, the gentle beating, and the morning chant you quietly sang, still echoing in the distance of your mind, and into the distance of the world around you . . .

Way hey . . . Way hey yah . . . Way hey yah ha . . . Way hey yah
All is Sacred . . .

All is Beautiful . . .
Way hey . . . Way hey yah . . . Way hey yah ha, way hey yah
Beauty is before me . . .
Beauty is behind me . . .
Beauty is above me . . .
Beauty is around me . . .
Beauty is within me . . .
Manitou is Beauty . . .
Manitou, Great Mystery . . .
Way hey . . . Way hey yah . . . Way hey yah ha, way hey yah

Your friend's focus remains fixed on the drum, but she's unable to hear the beat that still resonates within you. Your friend cannot hear the chanting, but even so, an energy lingers in the room and around the sacred space you have created, and an inkling of that feeling sparks your friend's sense of longing for the unknown experience. Seized by an overeager curiosity, she interjects into the silence, "Is that a turtle?" referring to the painted image on the drum. "Can I hold it?"

You glance at your friend, and smile. Then your gaze returns to the drum. "Yes," you respond with kindness, "but first, you must ask and thank turtle drum for her permission."

Crazy Horse

We hear what you say

One Earth one Mother

One does not sell the Earth

The people walk upon

We are the land

How do we sell our Mother

How do we sell the stars

How do we sell the air

—JOHN TRUDELL WAS AN AUTHOR, POET, ACTOR, MUSICIAN, AND POLITICAL ACTIVIST, KNOWN AS ONE OF THE GREAT INDIGENOUS MINDS OF OUR TIME. REJECTING WORDS THAT LABELED OR CATEGORIZED HIM, JOHN CONSIDERED HIMSELF A **HUMAN BEING**.

CHAPTER TWENTY-SIX

THE PRISON, THE PIPE, AND THE DRUM

It might have been the winter of 1977. This is my recollection of what happened.

Sometime before my telephone meeting with the warden, students and elders of Heart of the Earth Drum had sung at the prison powwow that the warden had been legally obliged to allow. The presence of the drum would resound and echo through the cold halls of the prison, the beats and songs preparing for another, even more dangerous event, one requested for a long time but denied, in my opinion, because it could empower the Native inmates to require the same respect for their beliefs as the Christians, the Jews, and the Muslims.

The warden did not want this. He claimed later on that an Indian inmate had dropped a hallucinogen in the warden's punch that day. It was described to me as a violent scene, where the warden had to be forcibly removed from the Indian gathering, swearing his hatred for Indians the whole time. Many of the prisoners disregarded the warden's vitriol, instead, imagining the big drum beating as they danced, and the sound and sight, terrifying him. Afterwards, the Indian prisoners believed that the warden hated them. I feel, that he hated them, in part, because, in a vulnerable moment, the drum may have touched his heart and, for an instant, he gained a rare insight into himself. He saw the Indian prisoners as men, fellow human beings, with a culture that his own was responsible for destroying. It was an instantaneous flash of understanding . . . I had seen this reaction before among such men, and I have seen it since. Their response has usually been violent, or hurtful.

I held the phone to my ear, trying not to absorb the poison words coming through the line. *Liars and thieves, dopers and dealers*, that's what the warden called the men who asked me to bring the pipe into the prison so they could pray like Indians. *Nothin' but liars and thieves! Dopers and dealers! Con artists!*

Then he said to me, *I'm working with official Indians and a certified medicine man. You're no medicine man.*

I never claimed to be, I said. *But I do keep a pipe, and these men asked to pray with this pipe. And they will.*

You're nothin' but a troublemaker, Horn. You're conspiring with other troublemakers, and I won't have it. They're nothin' but bullshit, and so are you! And then he cursed again . . . *No pipe! No goddamn drum!*

I sit in my chair now, nearly forty years later, at the side of the warrior's drum. I no longer have a stand for the old drum to elevate him to intensify his sound, so his weight leans against my leg. I keep him propped enough that his head of deerskin does not touch the floor. Near us, the pipe I carried into the prison long ago is close at hand.

As I hold the drumstick, wrapped in buffalo hair, buffalo skin covering the tip, I begin softly beating. [Softly beating . . .]

Thus the story unfolds to the beating of the warrior's drum . . .

And this is my telling . . .

The prison warden didn't want me or the pipe there. He contrived with others to keep us out. They called themselves Indians, too, using grant money to pay for administering the fees for such an event, and of course, a certified medicine man, an idea we had not heard of, to perform a "ceremony" in the prison—which, after all this time, hadn't happened. We didn't think it would ever happen. [One strong powerful beat on the warrior's drum!]

He didn't want the sacred pipe there . . . [Another strong beat!] He didn't want these men to have the choice . . . Nor to share in this sacred pipe ceremony. [Another powerful beat . . .] "Nothin' but liars and thieves," he called them. "Dopers and dealers!"

But the men were determined . . . [A strong beat . . .] They requested the pipe of their choice be brought to them. [Another thunderous beat . . . and another and another . . .]

As the beat steadies I close my eyes and call on my memory some more, for the story needs to be told . . .

I was teaching Indian students at South High School in Minneapolis at the time, part-time, Indian literature classes. [Continuous beating now . . .] Some of the students had relatives in that prison, brothers and uncles and such. Fathers. [One loud beat among the others . . . !] The men inside the prison chose the pipe I kept to be the first one. And this would not be easy . . . It was not easy. It was hard. I had to find the courage . . . [Still beating steadily . . . rhythmically . . .] I had to find the power within myself to help my people, I had to find the mettle to deal with this bully who was the warden . . . But the leaders of these men inside were strong . . . ! I was strong . . . ! And the pipe the men requested would not be denied entrance into that prison. This was my responsibility. [One loud beat among the others . . . !]

[Now imagine the steady drumming of my stick upon the warrior drum as I tell you this story . . . Imagine emphasizing a word, a thought, a moment, another louder beat . . . And maybe even two or three or four consecutively . . . *Boom! Boom! Boom! Boom!* Hear the beating of the drum in your mind as I tell the story! Feel the beating of this story in your heart! Tap your heel on the floor with the book in your hands. Tap your hand on the table or the arm of your chair.]

A circle of human beings had formed on the stage in the dimly lit and dismal prison auditorium. A circle! Nature's most powerful symbol! We had joked at the beginning of the ceremony, the men and me, trying to figure out which direction was east, the place of birth and rebirth. New beginnings. The place in the circle where the pipe begins the journey. "This truly is a place where the sun don't shine!" one of the older men said. And we laughed. But scanning the large room, we noticed the armed uniformed guards, weapons at the ready . . . and the government agents, weapons not so concealed under their suit jackets, and each of them interspersed among the seating and the doors . . .

On that day, not only were the Indian prisoners in that circle . . . [The beating of the drum where I sit now resounds . . . Boom, Boom, Boom] A few of their relatives and close friends came to visit, uncles and brothers, sisters and mothers, so the circle was big . . . [Boom] The circle was strong . . . [Boom] The circle of human beings filled the stage . . . [Boom] Maybe a hundred [Boom]. And as the ghosts began to intermingle, there were more . . .

[The beat of the drum becomes steady and rhythmic as I look back in time and I see . . .]

A lit braid of sweetgrass and me bathing in the smoke, swirling it all over and around the pipe, and passing it sunwise, to the left, the people of the circle did the same, cleansing themselves with the sweet fragrant braid of Mother Earth's hair. The scent so beautiful, so sacred, in this place of medieval hell on Earth . . .

And as we passed the pipe, each smoked and prayed, and we were momentarily transported from that dismal place of darkness and imprisonment into another world, and that pipe never went out . . . [Boom] Could hold not enough tobacco for maybe half a cigarette, but never went out . . . [Boom].

Instead, when the ceremony was ending . . . [the drum now near me, against my knee, on the floor responding to my steady beating, and the retelling of this story], and the pipe had traveled through the hands and hearts of the people back to me . . . a big puff of smoke entered the once stagnant air and formed a swirling cloud that rose out and up to go everywhere . . .

As I was putting the pipe back into the beaded white rabbit fur bundle, I heard the beating of a big drum from behind me, and I turned . . . [Boom!]

The prisoners had somehow gotten this drum and were singing and beating upon that grandfather, and it was so powerful . . . [Boom!] Powerful, I say . . . [Boom!] Like thunder . . . [Boom, Boom, and Boom!] Powerful like crashing waves . . . [Boom, Boom, Boom!] The room vibrated with that beating, and we danced. The prisoners danced. Their relatives danced. I danced. And the pipe wrapped in the bundle danced in my arms.

[Even now as I recount this story across time and space, the beating of the drum then I feel again, as I beat on the drum against my knee now, and I am in my mind—dancing too!]

While armed guards and agents surrounded us, and the hateful threats of the prison warden lurked in the dark crevices at that place, and the angered Indian officials, who may have lost out on some grant money, we simply floated away . . . Over the walls and electric wires and guard towers of the prison. Over the threats and anger, and then over the trees. Above the Earth we danced . . . [Boom!] Over the rivers we danced . . . Over the hills and prairie grasses we danced . . . away from that place of medieval misery. Up into the Sky . . . with the clouds we danced. Out into space and time with the Sun, with the Moon, with the Stars. The drumbeat and the singers' voices lifted us away from this horror of confinement . . .

And we danced . . . [Boom!]

And now my own drumbeat fades, as does a story woven of belief, bravery, love, and compassion, the will to survive into the Mystery, resonating in the warrior's drum at my side.

PART NINE

NOT ALWAYS SO
BLACK AND WHITE

With regard to ancient teachings . . . I can only share what I've learned. What makes sense to me. The infinitesimal that I have come to know is based on my vision and my dreams, and the precious fragments of acquired knowledge of past generations, some shared in books, some through conversations and observations. To rule out exceptions, or to say it has to be this way, or no way, I can't do that. I can only try and understand and use my intelligence . . .

CHAPTER TWENTY-SEVEN

HANDLING THE PIPE AND THE DRUM

A dream tells me . . .

At some point in my life, when I was in my late twenties, no doubt when I needed to hear it in this way, when I had been presented with a sacred pipe, I had a dream; and in the dream, it was made very clear that I should *not* mix, in any way, any substance but tobacco, or kinnikinnick (a form of Indian tobacco), when I was using the pipe, or handling anything sacred, like the drum. Nor should I *ever* be intoxicated when using either of them.

While it is true, that elders could teach me these things, and they had, it was from a dream, the kind of dream that makes you pay attention, or else, that would truly make me never want to challenge this teaching.

But I was young then, and I was learning that these particular teachings were for me, and that I may have little or no control over what others may say or do. We can mostly control only what we do. How we behave. How we live. And I had learned, along this way of the drum, that sometimes not all things and all teachings may be so black and white. Sometimes there are gray areas. Sometimes . . .

NO ALCOHOL/HONOR THE EARTH

When I was a teacher in the American Indian Movement survival schools, I experienced a powwow for the first time where alcohol was prohibited. Considering how alcohol has devastated Native communities, not to mention most other communities in this country, let us consider the words of Benjamin Franklin: "Rum is an agent of Providence," and that it may be "the design of Providence to extirpate these savages in order to make room for the cultivators of the earth." I was ready for this moment. Ironically, the name of the street in Minneapolis where all the "Indian bars" were clustered was Franklin Avenue. It was not far from where our school, Heart of the Earth, was located in a housing project.

And so, this was my first no alcohol, honor the Earth powwow. It took place several hours away from Minneapolis, deep in the Wisconsin forest. Armed AIM security guards wearing red berets greeted us as we turned off the paved two-lane highway and onto the rutted dirt road. They asked the driver and passengers of each vehicle if there was alcohol in the car. They asked who was in the car. Sometimes they opened the trunk and searched. We were in Cactus Jack's green Gremlin, as I recall, so there was no trunk, and we headed down the road.

It felt like I had stepped back in time a hundred years or more. Hearing the big drum and the singers in the distance and seeing the glow from the fires as we approached knowing no one was drinking or drunk, I felt safe and wonderful. All of us in the car must have been feeling the same. We were a great new nation emerging, and it seemed like nothing could stop us from reclaiming the past and grabbing hold of the future. I remember seeing, for the first time, dancers of all kinds but none were wearing numbers to designate that they were being judged in a competition for prize money. They were dancing to the drummers' singing for the Earth. They were dancing for life. This was a singing and drumming and dancing gathering of Indigenous people, and friends, to honor the Earth, and for three days and two nights that is exactly what we did there.

A SHOT GLASS RAISED AT THE DRUM

At another similar powwow on one of the reservations north of the city, not too long after honor the Earth, still in the early seventies, I was drawn close to a specific drum and singers. This drum felt especially strong and even unique as the singers who sung in Ojibway consisted of a circle of older men—men who had known struggle and heartache, men who had worked hard many years in their lives. That border dividing the two worlds of life and death shadowed their faces in the firelight.

I was young, in my mid-twenties then, and these elders were well into their fifties, sixties, and I think even seventies and eighties. Considering that the average life span of American Indian men back then was around fifty-four, they were old. Most of them had experienced what it is to be Indigenous in ways I hadn't. Most of them had lived through world wars. I had had some battles, but my biggest one was how to best deal with the overwhelming pain that tormented me at gravesites when I watched or helped bury too many of our people who were drunk when they died. Too many young victims of car crashes. Too many of our people succumbing to shootings, stabbings, fights in bar parking lots, freezing on their way home, suicide. Alcohol was always involved. It almost claimed me.

I grew to hate alcohol.

And, yet, I had noticed at this most special and powerful drum of elder men, that at some point before their turn came to sing the next song, one of the men would fill a bit of a plastic cup or a shot glass of whiskey for each man sitting in an old lawn chair or folding metal chair in the circle at the drum. They did this with discrimination, though, quietly, subtly. Like a ceremony of sorts. Before they drank, they raised their glasses a bit, said something in Ojibway to one of their own who had fallen. Then they poured some of the whiskey in their cups or glasses on the ground as an offering, and drank down the rest.

Their drumming and singing echoed between worlds in the night.

What is the World, if not Magic; what is Magic, if not the World?

—THE BOOK OF CEREMONIES

A MAGICAL BOY, PERHAPS; A MAGICAL MOMENT, FOR CERTAIN

It was at the University of Minnesota that I had experienced the largest gathering of Native Americans I had ever seen up until that moment in my life. This was an enormous powwow. At least, that's how I remember it. Despite the number of people attending, I know that I was feeling utterly alone, even though so many times I was greeted and comforted by the kind faces of elders who knew me and some who didn't know me, and young people who were my students at Heart of the Earth. Oftentimes, the young ones would race up to me and, filled with energy, sometimes out of breath, always with excitement, they'd say, Hello. I remember how the dancers seemed electric with colorful feathers and beadwork of all shapes and designs, the drums thunderous, and the singing haunting and evocative. It was all wonderful!

Even though I was alone.

So I just found a spot where I could sit on the floor and, as a part of the grand circle of watchers that circled the entire gym, absorbed all the beauty of being Indigenous that was around me.

Then, during one of the songs, something strange happened, and I will never forget that moment.

My eye caught sight of a young boy, about seven or eight years old. He was dressed in exquisite clothes and fine feathers of all kinds of birds, almost flying like a bird himself, looking directly at me and moving in dance to the beating drum and singing. He flew, dancing, right toward me. He was a beautiful boy. The kind of Indian boy Edward Curtis would've wanted to photograph—the kind of Indian boy tourists might see on a postcard in a trading post somewhere in Oklahoma, and want to send home to show they'd been in Indian country.

This wasn't just any beautiful Indian child; he was magic. He was, as the Lakota might say, wakan.

I noticed that other onlookers were observing what was happening, and some looked in our direction in awe; others were smiling. As he danced closer to me I felt this sacred connection with him—too sacred to impose any thoughts upon it or even to try to describe it. It did seem otherworldly. He remained there, this beautiful Indigenous boy, right in front of me, his dark eyes looking at mine, his face serious and kind, and as that song played on the drum, he never stopped dancing in front of me.

Then the drumming and singing stopped, and he was gone. Just like that! I didn't know what had happened, but I knew something of beauty and mystery had acknowledged me.

I felt honored and humbled and deeply moved. I felt special. I felt myself to be a good man, despite my loneliness. A gift of the magical boy who danced a dance before me . . .

DRUMMING FOR EUGENIA IN CHURCH

My dear friend Eugenia was at home, and she was dying. Her companion had phoned and said that she had asked for me to bring the drum to her deathbed and drum for her. The idea of losing her was almost too much to bear. Eugenia was older than me. In several ways, she reminded me of Uncle Nip, even sharing a Celtic-inspired spirit and the same last name, Sanders. I mean, what are the odds? She had a way of cutting through the bullshit of life, and her opinions could be piercing, even hurtful. She had a tendency to overindulge when it came to alcohol, which, as for most of us, leads to some unpleasant situations. But she was a sister/friend when I needed one.

And, what was truly exceptional about her, was the pottery she created. She once told me that she loved to work with clay because she loved the Earth. She called the Earth, Mother. She taught pottery classes in her studio occasionally, and was an extraordinary teacher. And she was the kind of Irish who still believed in the old Celtic ways. That included her spiritual relationship with being Indigenous and her love for the drum.

As my wife Amy and I prepared for a night of drumming and assisting Eugenia's transition into the Great Change, a hurricane hit. Tropical rains in the day make it almost impossible to see beyond your front door. The rains flooded the streets quickly. Living by the sea, even the peaceful gulf becomes a powerful, wild force without any kind of human control, and the ocean roars, *Stay away from me!*

When tropical rains come at night, it becomes almost impossible to drive anywhere. Then add waves of wind that take down strong trees and power lines, and rip off roofs, and we weren't leaving the house. Eugenia would die during that hurricane, the drumming she would hear would not be coming from the hand drum I had hoped to bring to her, but it would come in the form of the heavy tropical rain, beating on the roof of her small house. No drumming could have been more powerful.

After Eugenia's body was cremated, her companion phoned again. She asked if I would bring the drum to the Unitarian church where there would be a memorial service held in Eugenia's honor. Though Eugenia was not a Christian, certain churches practice tolerance that others do not. After her death, her companion, drawing on the camaraderie and acceptance of the Unitarians, and those closest to Eugenia, had taken charge of arrangements.

I had always felt there should be no mixing of organized religious dogma and Indigenous understandings. I had never imagined I would be singing a song on the drum to the Great Mystery for a person I loved inside a church.

But, love is of the Mystery, and I was getting older and, I'd like to think, wiser. I was learning that things aren't always so black and white—the *it's got to be this way or no way* kind of mentality. Sometimes, we need to forge a compromise. I was learning all along the journey in this Great Mystery of a universe, wide as daylight and bright as starlight, that there could always be exceptions.

Amy and I attended Eugenia's memorial service that day. When I was invited up to the altar, with the powerful hand drum, I drummed and sang for my dear sister friend with every cell of my being. The sound of an Indigenous drum filled the church for the first time in the building's history, the song in my voice touching the Great Mystery in all things, and reaching out and into the other world. I want to think that in ways as old as there has been grieving in the world, the spirit of Eugenia's life felt the drum and that the song of our loss and love for her helped give that spirit peace.

POCAHONTAS
Susan Deer Cloud

December 2012 marked my life circling back to its beginning, although little did I know when the first starlike snows took pity on the leafless land I was a mere four moons away from returning to the Catskill town I grew up in. Already I was seeing John, an old lover of mine from the last hurrah of the 1960s, which is why on the night of this story I was riding with him to a Dutch Reformed church outside Rosendale, New York. Understand, my lover, whom I called Raised-By-Wolves, had a degree from MIT and mocked religions for being unscientific if not perpetrators of war, and I was a Catskill Indian who had developed a fierce aversion to organized Christianity because of its oppression and murders of Indigenous people, wise women, and others unable to nail their asses to a hard wooden pew for life. Yet there we were, watching glints of snowflakes burst into tiny flames in the headlights of our car knifing through the cold dark to a church.

As it turned out, Raised-By-Wolves had a twenty-something friend, Jim, who was a member of Virginia's Pamunkey tribe that Pocahontas belonged to. For me, meeting Jim was magical, since my mother first explained our Indian "blood" by pressing a brown doll into my arms and saying her name was Pocahontas.

"Pocahontas is like you," she explained. "You must always protect her, Susie, and make sure nothing bad happens to her."

Jim, a kind and mellow man, had two young sons and a daughter, T.T., who emanated the same bright and mischievous spirit that Pocahontas possessed before she was kidnapped. Jim's father, Nick, minister at the Dutch Reformed church, practiced his Pamunkey traditions along with following the roving Jesus who at best thought like an Indian. Nick hosted monthly Native American potluck gatherings in the church basement, and Jim thought that I might wish to be a part of it.

John eased into the church parking lot and I grabbed the venison lasagna I had made for the potluck. It tickled me to make an Italian dish mixed with an Indian food staple, deer meat, given how many Italians had played Indians in cowboys-and-Indians movies. I bore the lasagna through the falling snow with a big grin crossing my face, snow crystals delicate hors d'oeuvres on my tongue. Jim greeted us, smiling, at the door, and introduced me to his father and mother who were equally generous in welcoming us. We cried "Hello" to Jim's sons and to T.T. who nearly flew up to us in a fringed blue shawl embroidered with wild roses.

Soon Nick invited everyone to get in line for the food, elders first. Raised-By-Wolves and I hung back in order to let the old people mosey ahead of us, until someone said, "Elders first. You two can get your food now." My lover, whom I still sometimes saw as the boy-man of my flower child past, smirked at me: He still liked to joke that I was the "hot chick." I squinted at him. We elders, who apparently had entered into our second teenage-hood and forgot we had hair the color of the night snow, burst into laughter. Raised-By-Wolves, true to his Indian name and nature, dashed like Santa's reindeer ahead of me, scooping food into a miniature mountain on his plate. I was happy to see he was embracing Indian culture.

After dinner and after Nick conducted a private ceremony, Jim, his sons and other men brought out a great drum and sat in a circle around it. When the drumming began in that underground place in that snowstorm before Christmas, we all stood listening mutely and even shyly for a while, the deep sounds of the drumming carrying us back across the centuries to before the invasions and genocide. Back to before Pocahontas became a political pawn who experienced what so many Indigenous girls would eventually experience, including marriage to a white man, loss of one's homeland, and giving birth to a new Indian, the "mixed blood."

Jim's daughter skipped over to me, blue shawl swirling in the basement air like a patch of spring sky, black hair sparking out subtle rainbows beneath the fluorescent lights.

"Susan, Susan," she lilted into my musings, "come dance with me!"

Her small hand grabbing mine, she tugged me out to the center of the room, whirling around to the drumbeats, slow to their slow, faster to their faster. My new-found elder status wasn't going to get me out of dancing with this exuberant girl who always made me suspect she was an avatar of Pocahontas. So I began dancing with T.T. as her father, grandfather, and brothers bowed their heads intently to the vibrating drumskin, drumsticks flashing up and down like eagle wings. T.T. whirled, wilder and wilder, as I flashed on the bullies who insisted our freedom was "savage," cut our hair, and bullied us into becoming two-faced forked-tongues, instead of the poetry-tongued people of trusting faces we originally were. But on that winter's night my young friend and I danced all the brutality away, she in her flowered Sky shawl and I in my blood-red poncho, girl and woman with long unbound hair and near breathless truth songs evoked by the drum and Mother Earth's heart still beating strong.

Long time ago I promised my mother I would protect Pocahontas and not let anything bad happen to her. Dancing with Jim's daughter, I vowed I would do my best to protect T.T.'s shine and not let anything destroy her and all the other "mixed blood" children of Pocahontas.

—SUSAN DEER CLOUD, AWARD-WINNING INDIGENOUS POET AND AUTHOR OF SEVERAL WORKS, INCLUDING *BEFORE LANGUAGE*, *CAR STEALER*, AND *THE LAST CEREMONY*.

PART TEN

MAKING TIME/FINDING SPACE

Where do we go to beat the drum?

Living in a civilized world, a world of technology and machines, where civilized man, who thinks himself superior to all other beings, has in his civilized mind separated himself from Nature and embraced his right to wasteful excess, to brutal conduct, to deliberate abuse of the environment he cannot escape . . . where Earth exists to serve, as She is altered and changed to suit what he craves cannot last . . .

Where do we go in a civilized world

where man-unkind does not kill himself and beyond his needs,

for sport and amusement other life forms,

for greed . . . and for God and for Allah and Jehovah

and in the names of Jesus and Mohammed and organized religions, for Communism, and Socialism, for Capitalism, for other people's lands and resources, and ultimately kills en masse, where in his civilized mind even the Earth is not alive?

Where do we go . . . to be alone . . .

to sing, to pray, to reconnect to Nature and to the inner peace of Wak-kon-tah in each of us?

Where do we go with the drum? How do we find a sacred space?

Where do we go?

CHAPTER TWENTY-EIGHT

MAKING TIME . . .

When he was a professor, my uncle once told a creative writing student, who was frustrated about not being able to find time to write, just what to do. The student ran down a litany of work- and chore-related activities that prevented her from having any personal time to sit down and write.

My uncle Nip's response, spoken decades ago, still resonates in my nearly seventy-year-old brain, as I too have struggled to find time: time to write; time to be peaceful; time to be grateful; time to drum.

His answer? You make the time.

CHAPTER TWENTY-NINE
FINDING SPACE/SOMEWHERE TO DRUM

If the drum has been, or is now becoming, a part of this path you walk, then finding where one goes to commune through, and with, the drum, has been a part of that journey. We may have discovered which are the best places and times for us to go to drum, where we can go to sing if we need to, or want to. Sometimes, quietly, in our space, we have learned how to do this in deeply primal ways, not grabbing the attention of our civilized neighbors in the civilized world, and not intruding on the natural world, either. If our paths have guided us to more natural areas, our drumming ritual has probably become a part of the nature of the place we have chosen. However, if making our way to this drum path has been a recent self-discovery, then the challenge can be more difficult. In either case, finding the time and space to drum, I have realized certain things: No matter where I am, especially when the need to drum arises, I've always tried to be aware of the world around me. I ask permission, and state my gratitude.

And so, the need has arisen, and I want to hold the drum. It could be the solstice of summer, the full moon of strawberries. It could be the birth of a grandchild. It could be the suffering of a friend. Then I ask myself, *Why have I come to this place? How must I explain my presence?* To whom, and to what, shall I be grateful for this moment? Sometimes I sit on the floor or in a chair in our home and I drum. Sometimes I close the windows; sometimes I don't. What I often search for are the moments that are peaceful and quiet, when the immediate world around me is most likely not to be filled with the vibrations of machines or cars or sirens, or even people's voices. And, even if the noise of civilized living occurs, I am in another state of existence, and the drum and I will outlast it. I know my patience will help me find the peace in between, and my experience has taught me that if my intent is pure, the space will come, and it may even be created by my beating on the drum . . . It always has—no matter where.

If I am fortunate enough to discover a place in nature, away from the noises and energies of the city, I must ask: What about the other life forms where I choose to be with my drum? Would I have their permission? Would the trees mind my drumming, my singing? The rocks? The water? The plants? The animals? The tiny insects? So many things to consider, and always remaining humble in the process. Still, I need to drum. First, I must say to all beings around me, *Thank you for permission and all that you do. And thank you for allowing me to be here and for all you have given. Thank you, Indigenous ancestors, who have kept the drums in the world. Thank you, Spirit of this place.*

We don't have to beat so the whole world can hear it; we can beat with our stick or our hand, depending on how we are taught. I drum until the sound synchronizes with my heart, and the heart of the Earth, and even deeper to the heart of the universe, and I am traveling in the Mystery, and I am singing . . . and I enter, and for these precious moments I exist on an alternate plane in the world, more like a separate reality.

CHAPTER THIRTY

A SENSE OF PURPOSE: WHY ARE WE HERE IN THIS CIRCLE? WHY DO I NEED TO DRUM?

It has been said that everything has a purpose. Wind and ocean and rivers and streams and lakes and ponds. Each has a purpose. Trees and plants and flowers and grasses. Each has a purpose. Animals have a sense of purpose. Birds have a sense of purpose. Bees and butterflies have purpose. Even ants somehow know their purpose. It seems that only humans have forgotten.

Oh, but some will insist they have a purpose. To bring Jesus to the heathens! To create a world of Islam! To make as much money as possible. To have a big home. Several big homes! To be in positions of power over others. Yes, after self-reflection, many might admit that these are the purposes for which they exist. Some even die to perpetuate this way of life. Others send others to die. What they can't say is how such a purpose brings us into harmony with our environment. How does such a purpose allow us to show our love and respect and gratitude for life? How does such a purpose honor not just the rights of human beings, but the natural rights of all things?

I have been taught that women have a primary purpose. Most women are born with it. It is the ability to give birth and/or to nurture life. A woman may discover other ways to contribute to the world through another purpose, but she still is born with one. She is empowered to choose whether to fulfill her purpose in this way.

Man, however, has no such innate purpose. He must seek his purpose for being on this Earth. I have been told that seeking a vision, the arduous ritual of denying the body for enlightenment of the spirit, is one way a man seeks his primary purpose, a purpose that will guide him, even provide him with the medicine that could help him to help his people—to make a contribution. And there it is, to make a contribution.

I have read from the book of a renowned Indigenous elder who wrote that back in the day, *A man without a vision was only a half man, someone who could not be trusted.*

And so, since everything in nature has a purpose, why am I here with my drum?

CHAPTER THIRTY-ONE

MIDNIGHT OF THE DAWN OF OUR MARRIAGE: THE DRUM AND THE LOVE SONG

Our relatives had provided a sunset reception when Amy and I were married many years ago on the pipe alone together at dawn on the beach. We loved our families, but this moment was between Amy and me and the pipe, and the dawn star, and warm air and lightening Sky, and rising Sun, and the last lingering stars hanging over our beloved Mother, the Ocean. We did this at the edge of night on the new moon of the morning of the summer solstice, connecting our marriage forever to natural time.

Amy's mom and relatives and friends gave a wonderful evening reception, and my brother Danuuka offered tobacco and cedar and addressed Wakonda (the Great Mystery) in the Ponca language, which he translated into English before a small fire, waving an eagle-feathered fan through the scented smoke. My children, who had grown to young adults and had lost their mom to cancer years ago, were now transitioning into a new family, with a new mother. A kind and loving mother, as I imagine any birth mother would have wanted for her children. And our friends, Amy's mom and dad, and her stepdad and her stepmom, and other relatives, each in his or her own way were participating in this ceremony. And though our marriage had taken place at dawn, with that sunset ceremony my kindhearted brother Danuuka had brought each person who was important in our lives into our circle of love, giving everyone a sense of inclusion. That was truly thoughtful and beautiful. He had been attentive to the feelings of others, and we would be ever grateful to him for that. But that was Danuuka, and so much of why we loved him.

Afterwards, we feasted on good food, and luscious fruits, and then we had our wedding dance to Foreigner's song, "Waiting for a Girl Like You." The merging of two worlds with joy!

Something, however, had remained undone. I had a wedding song, too, a love song, just for Amy. But I needed the hand drum. I needed a private place. A sacred space. *Where to drum my love song to my love?*

> *They say, Be aware, be patient, be pure in intent,*
> *and the moment will come,*
> *and you will know when and where*
> *it is right to drum . . .*

The family and friends had gathered at a beach resort, and it was getting late. I left for a few moments and suddenly appeared before my extraordinary wife, holding my hand drum. This drum had been in many ceremonies. Ceremonies to help heal the heart. Ceremonies to heal the mind. Ceremonies to heal the physical body. The hand drum had traveled with me to distant places. This hand drum helped me travel from the floor in my small house to other worlds and into the universe. And into my deepest self.

I stood holding the new buffalo drumstick that Amy had given me earlier that month, and I smiled at Amy, this beauty, named in Dakota Oieihake Win (Last Word Woman), and I whispered, "Will you walk with me?"

Just before we reached the shore, we sat on the sand. By this time we were far enough away from the hotel that conversations and music could no longer be a distraction. Our senses keened to the warm night air of the solstice, the darkness of the night, and the ocean's luminescent waves, reaching up to touch us, and to love us. I explained that I had a song I wanted to sing for her, *for us*. She smiled so sweetly, it wrapped around me, and my love for Last Word Woman overcame any nervousness I was feeling, the drum making certain I was engaged in the special moment of the song as soon as I began softly beating . . .

Soft and steady, until the rhythm for the song felt right, I began singing:

Ooooo . . . cean . . . Ooooo . . . cean . . . Ooooo . . . cean . . .

Waaaay . . . heyyy . . . yah, waaaay . . . heyyyy . . . yah

And while I was singing I could hear the small waves feeling the shore, extending up to touch us, and the song and the beating of the drum seemed in loving harmony and rhythm with the ocean, and I chanted between the words the feelings that love conjures, the energy of the incoming tide . . .

Ooooo . . . cean . . . Ooooo . . . cean . . . Ooooo . . . cean . . .

Waaaay . . . heyyy . . . yah, waaaay . . . heyyyy . . . yah...

Dolllllll . . . phin . . . Dolllllll . . . phin . . . Waaaay . . . heyyyy . . .

yah, Waaaaayheyyyy . . . yah

I sang the song four times to the beat of the drum. On the fourth time, the song faded . . . The ocean is Amy. She is that much love. I am the dolphin secure in that love, and in need of her embrace. And so, that night of the day we married, I sang my love song to Oieihake Win. We had created our space. The drum created our space. Any distractions from relatives and friends, or beach walkers, or things that happen in the world of tourists, disappeared from our consciousness, and there was only us and the soft beating of the drum and the song carried in the sound of the waves, the song and the stars and the ocean, and maybe a dolphin hearing the song. Or even baby turtles emerging from the sand not far down the beach at the base of the dunes, heading toward the water, toward their own embrace of the ocean—all hearing the song . . .

CHAPTER THIRTY-TWO
A PURPOSE FOR THE DRUMMING

DRUMS ALONG THE KLONDIKE
Ellyn Lee as told to Sarah McCracken

A gentleman named Eskimo Joe was going around speaking to different churches and Ellyn Lee's aunt and uncle invited him to stay at their house while he was in town. He started talking to their son Robert while he was there and he told the parents that Robert was the most psychic child he had ever known. He asked if he could take Robert back to his people to train him. So Ellyn Lee's cousin Robert, a young teenager at the time, went with Eskimo Joe to the Klondike for the summer where they assisted him with his psychic growth.

When he left that summer, they sent him home in a kayak and they drummed him home. They drummed messages all along the way to other Inuit communities to let them know he was coming. It took several days and nights for him to reach his destination. At every stop, there were First Nations to meet him and he would stay overnight with them and then they would prepare him for the journey the next day, following the drumming until he got to the transportation that would take him back to America.

—ELLYN LEE, BELOVED TEACHER FOR MANY YEARS.
SARAH MCCRACKEN, HER DAUGHTER, ACTRESS AND TEACHER.

CHAPTER THIRTY-THREE

THE REASON FOR OUR GATHERING

We need to agree on the purpose of the gathering. Is it to reconnect to our spiritual consciousness? Is it to address with love another human being? Is it to address from our beating hearts and drums our gratitude for the Earth and Sky and Moon and Sun, and the Great Mystery? And for the very life that sustains us? Of course. But we may simply need to reconnect to that part of ourselves that is spirit. Maybe we are hurting. Maybe we are just grateful. Do we beat our drums in prayer for healing for ourselves and others? Is it to pray for peace within ourselves and in the world? Are we drumming together to help a spirit just separated from the physical body at death, and to help keep those grieving hearts, suffering from the loss, beating strong? What is the purpose of our gathering? Why am I here in this circle of drums? Maybe I don't even know. Maybe something just beckoned me here, something I can't explain. But I just need to be here with the drum. I need to touch the spirit within me that gives me life. I need to get in touch with what is most important in my life . . .

THE WAY OF THE POWWOW

Expressions of song, dance, art, and community, centered around the drum, seem to call up our deepest feelings of connection. The drumbeat, the heartbeat of the powwow gathering, sinks into the Earth and is felt in the feet and body. The rhythm is also lifted up into the air, into the Sky. The ancestral spirits of a place and of the people are felt to gather to witness. How this works is undefined and unspoken. It is felt and understood, a reflection of the very heartbeat of Mother Earth . . . something we cannot help but respond to!

—PAMELA BENNETT IS A RESPECTED ELDER, ARTIST, DESIGNER, AND CRAFTSPERSON INSPIRED BY THE SYMBOLIC ART OF THE MISSISSIPPIAN MOUND BUILDERS.

HEARTBEAT

Pamela Bennett

As soon as I stepped into the dance circle with its slowly clockwise rotating stream of dancers, the feeling seemed to come up from the ground. Stepping with small measured footsteps and bending at the knees, as befit the female traditional dancers, soon my steps seemed to be floating above the ground. My thoughts turned to the ancestors, mine and those of this location of the powwow gathering.

Already familiar with the sense of dislocation produced by the rhythmic reverberations of a large powwow drum at the other events, I was not quite prepared for the powerful impressions I felt while dancing to the drum, together with others.

Each beat and song is played simultaneously. As many men as can fit sit on folding chairs around the drum. Men around the drum, women around the men, women around a cook-fire . . . all producing nourishment for a gathering of people.

A powwow drum measures up to three feet across, sits on a custom-made, low wooden stand, and is constructed of cedar or another special wood. Slats are fastened together in a circle, an elk, moose, or buffalo hide stretched across and tethered to the frame. A drum is honored by the keeper, has its own blanket, is heated by fire before use to increase the depth of its timbre, and is prayed over with tobacco offerings. The drum holds and conveys a united voice of the people—those who sit around the drum, the singers, each with his own drumstick.

Whether those in the sacred circle are there to celebrate culture, satisfy curiosity, dance, or merely observe, the drum's voice seems to call in and satisfy a most primitive need felt in the soul, a need to belong to the greater Mystery, as expressed by the reverberations of a simultaneously played drum in a social setting. The drum reflects the very heartbeat of Mother Earth from the depths of the planet core, brings it up and out into the sunlight and up into the Sky World, as sound.

This is the meaning of the sacred drum and the sacred circle, where we can match our own heartbeat to something so much larger than ourselves, somehow finding that we are part of what connects Earth and Sky.

CHAPTER THIRTY-FOUR

DISRUPTION OF THE DRUMMING CIRCLE

On a private speck of shoreline in a wide expanse of white sandy beach one evening at sunset, a take-a-deep-breath-and-release-slowly time of day, a group of teenagers heckled and harassed a drumming circle. The circle had been meeting once a month the last Thursday evening at sunset on this spot. The people in the circle came from various backgrounds and were of different ages and stages in life. Each brought a drum, each in his and her own way reaching back to ancestral tribal ways. But the teenagers, who were not taught or inclined to appreciate and respect others, disrupted the drumming circle to such an extent that the people who had gathered with their drums couldn't feel at ease, even in this exquisite place. The drumming ceased and the circle was broken.

To my knowledge, it has not come back.

CHAPTER THIRTY-FIVE

THE RUNAWAY DRUM

The circle at the Native gathering wasn't broken by government agents, religious extremists, or the police. It was broken by the people, by the spirits that we conjure. It was broken by what we didn't listen to. What we didn't do . . . What we did and what we needed to do. But, most importantly, the lesson of a drum . . .

HOW (NOT!) TO TAKE PROPER CARE OF A DRUM AND BEATER
Evan Pritchard

A long time ago I was invited to travel out west to a traditional Native American gathering in the mountains to set up a tent and present some traditional drum songs sung in the old Algonquin languages. It was called the Screaming Eagle Drum Circle Annual Powwow. It turned out to be one of the strangest events I ever attended, but I learned a big lesson: that the "medicine" of the drum is real and not something to play games with. I learned that when you drum for a gathering with strangers, it's a good idea to smudge yourself and your drum before you get started, so that the wrong kind of "medicine" doesn't take over.

I brought my drum and my beater in a drum bag that had been sewn by an

Ojibway medicine woman, and I always felt they were safe in that bag. I was wrong. I should have smudged the bag when I entered. I should have cleansed the drum head with tobacco offerings. I should have blessed the drum in the name of Kitchi Manitou (another word for Great Spirit).

I noticed that a number of people started arguing with each other over simple matters. There was a strange man who came into the crowd, a man with one eye and painted from head to toe, carrying a war club. He seemed angry, but spoke words of peace, and as he spoke he used a form of "Indian" sign language I'd never seen. Soon, a few fistfights broke out. I was sharing my tent with others and strangers came into my tent and started rummaging through the trade objects, including my belongings. A man came into my tent, saying I had stolen his rifle, but I didn't know who he was or what he was talking about. I told the master of ceremonies that something was wrong, and that we all needed to be careful, but he disagreed. He said he had everything under control.

I brought my drum bag out to the speakers' blanket, but when I looked inside, my drum beater was gone. It was a Mi'kmaq drum and both the drum head and beater were made from moose hide. I belong to a "Moose Clan," and a Mi'kmaq warrior had made the drum for me many years earlier. I had used them for decades without a problem. They were part of my "drum medicine," and I had planned to sing some songs that would lift the energy. In the crazy atmosphere of that gathering, I thought someone had taken my beater. I looked around and all the various drum groups had beaters, but they were the wrong kind and were all in use in some way or another. I had to ask to be switched with another performer, and was granted that permission. I kept looking and could not find the beater. One of the drum groups offered me a long stick from the field drum, but it meant that one of their singers would have to sit it out. I said no. I wanted my drumstick!

I had some tribal history books I was showing some people, and I laid them out on a blanket for visitors to look at just inside the tent. During the search for my stick, I suddenly felt completely exhausted and had to lie down. In fact, I passed out. Just as suddenly a big storm blew in from out of nowhere, with a fierce wind that drove bucketsful of cold rain sideways into my tent, and all over me and my books. They were ruined within seconds. Now my clothes were drenched and my drum bag was soaking wet. It was a wake-up call. Just as quickly the storm disappeared and once again the skies were clear. Then the local sheriff arrived, responding to reports of a "crazy Indian" running around with a gun threatening to kill someone who owed him money. The man they were going after was not the same man who had confronted me about the rifle, it was the one-eyed man, the one talking about peace. He denied the charges.

They asked me again to sing some songs to calm the people, and offered me a whole array of wonderful hand drums, adorned with incredible paintings, and with feathers hanging from the tethers. I refused. My teachers had always said it was disrespectful to hit a traditional hand drum with your hand; always use a stick! I held my ground.

There seemed to be only one thing to do. I told them I was going home, and went to place my drum back in the bag, and there was my drumstick in plain sight. Did someone return it? Or was it right there all along, hidden by some sorcerer's spell? As soon as I stood up with the beater in my hand the master of ceremonies said, "Go up there and play, fer God's sakes! We've waited long enough!"

As it was called the "Screaming Eagle" Powwow and a lot of people had been screaming all day, I performed a number of eagle songs and was well received, but a lot of the crowd had already left to escape the storm. I then packed up my gear and placed them in my old car, and decided that my drum needed a healing. I placed the drum beater inside the drum and placed the drum in the trunk of the car and drove away.

. . . .

As evening began to fall, I drove into the mountains, looking for a place to do a real ceremony to heal my drum. I often prefer to make my offerings into waterfalls, or at least streams, as our ancestors did, so I went looking for one. On the way down the other side of that mountain, I found what I was looking for—a huge waterfall falling steeply from a great height. There was a small space to park my car, right near the edge of the great chasm, which the waterfall had carved out over millions of years. There was a cliff at the edge, a sheer drop, but no fence to keep people safe. I wondered if someone or something had placed an angry spirit being into my drum beater so that I could not sing songs to challenge the malevolent spirits that had taken over the powwow. I knew just the ceremony to drive it out.

When I opened the trunk I was in for a surprise. The drum, with the beater still inside, flew upwards and out, flying like an angry eagle, right past my face. I watched in amazement as it flipped midair from a horizontal position to a vertical one. As it floated downwards in a long arc it touched down on the Earth on its side, and began rolling downhill like a giant wagon wheel. I watched as if in a trance as it rolled merrily down the hill toward the edge of the ravine. For a moment everything unfolded in slow motion. As it rolled, it made a sound I will never forget, like distant thunder in the mountains, almost as if the voice of the Trickster were talking through the drum head. That little Trickster spirit wanted to get clean away, but if that drum went over the edge I would never find it again.

Suddenly my heart was beating like a drum. I flew into action, racing toward the edge of the ravine with a speed that can only be summoned in life-threatening circumstances. Running toward the edge of oblivion was not something I was accustomed to, but I did not want to lose that drum. Just as my Mi'kmaq moose drum was about to fly off into space, I slid and dived and reached out for the runaway drum, grabbing one of the tethers with my fingers and pulling the drum back to safety. My Little League training as a shortstop had never been more useful than at that moment. I was then finally able to give that instrument the cleansing and smudging that it needed. I tossed many tobacco offerings into the abyss that evening as the sun was setting, and asked Creator to teach me to be more careful about the medicine. Later, I asked the Great Spirit to enter into that drum beater and awaken it in service to Kitchi Manitou so that no other troublemakers could enter it, in an attempt to prevent the healing songs from being sung. It worked. I have never had a problem since.

—EVAN PRITCHARD IS AN ALGONQUIN SCHOLAR, PROFESSOR, POET, AND AUTHOR OF SEVERAL BOOKS, FROM MEMOIR (*NO WORD FOR TIME*) TO HISTORY (*NATIVE NEW YORKERS*).

CHAPTER THIRTY-SIX

SPACE AND TIME

Sometimes the spirit within us stirs our primal need and takes hold of our minds as we live our lives in a civilized world. And sometimes in the middle of the chaos, we find ourselves with others who feel the same need passed on through their own ancestral blood . . .

MANY HEARTS, ONE RHYTHM
Dawn Bednar

When my husband and I opened a store a couple hours from our Tampa Bay home, I was stuck in Orlando on business far more often than I liked. One occasion fell on a full moon, a time of sacred acknowledgment for Pagans, so I'd brought my drum, hoping to find a circle and some like-minded others. A popular vegan restaurant I'd been wanting to check out had one listed so with djembe in hand, I headed over.

Now, if you were to ask me, I'd tell you how nonjudgmental I am, so when I pulled into the parking lot and judged the whole scene, I forced myself to at least get out of the car before discounting any value.

In a congested area, surrounded by the noise of the city, I pushed aside my claustrophobia as I claimed a seat on the concrete wall surrounding the courtyard. It might have seemed cozy on a cold night but instead felt overcrowded as no connective thread joined the diverse group of people milling about in isolated clusters. The din of conversation had the vibe of a club, as a couple hipsters strummed Neil Young on pricey Gibsons (seriously?), causing me to wonder if Brie and Chardonnay were being served. Jaded youth, their wrists gauntleted in beaded bracelets, tapped on their drums as if tapping on their desk in boredom while the new agers chatted, and scattered displaced individuals peered out from their low self-esteem. With nothing else to do, I figured I'd give it one glass of tea before declaring it a bust, so I placed my drum between my knees and waited to see how the scene evolved. The moon rising over the trees was radiant and pulsing with energy, so at least there was that.

A shift was collectively perceived when three dreadlock-crowned young men emerged from a vintage green van and started hastily unloading other djembes and also Bodhrans. Running on hippie time, they offered apologetic smiles as they claimed their space in the center and their hands fell fast into a harmonic rhythm. Cigarettes were extinguished, conversations dwindled with the smoke, and the hipsters set aside their guitars as drums were lifted to join the beat. Not bestowed with musical skills, like so many others, I always feel a bit awkward in the first moments as my palms seek out the tones from skin and wood, but that's the beginning of the magick, medicine, and sacredness of the drum. It doesn't matter. The consciousness of the beat moves through my heart-space, and despite my inadequacies as a percussionist, my hands fall, unaware, into my own imperfectly perfect rhythm, blending in miraculous harmony with the others.

The things that connect us are most sacred. A lover's touch, laughter, a song, a dance; all rituals of unity and so, too, pure and primal is the drum. Her heartbeat, our heartbeat, the Heartbeat.

The traffic and the city vanished and the space became ample as the accelerating pulse coursed through me. Around me, some eyes were open, and some were closed, meditative and trancelike as palms, tappers, and cloth-wrapped sticks pounded all of our imperfections into a thing of beauty that filled the night. My hands were stinging, but I didn't pause or wipe away the sweat as the tempo spiraled upward, carrying with it our prayers, our dreams; our frenzied tribal souls. There was nothing but the ancient beat. Nothing but the drum.

And then, as if a conductor waved "Cut," all fell silent under the Goddess's glow. I met the smiles of strangers who seemed less so now. Souls awakened by the vibration shimmered with more truth as, through panting breaths, we chugged bottled water and waited for the next unwritten song to begin.

—DAWN BEDNAR, WRITER, FORMER WOLF AND WOLF-DOG RESCUER,
AND STANDING ROCK WATER PROTECTOR.

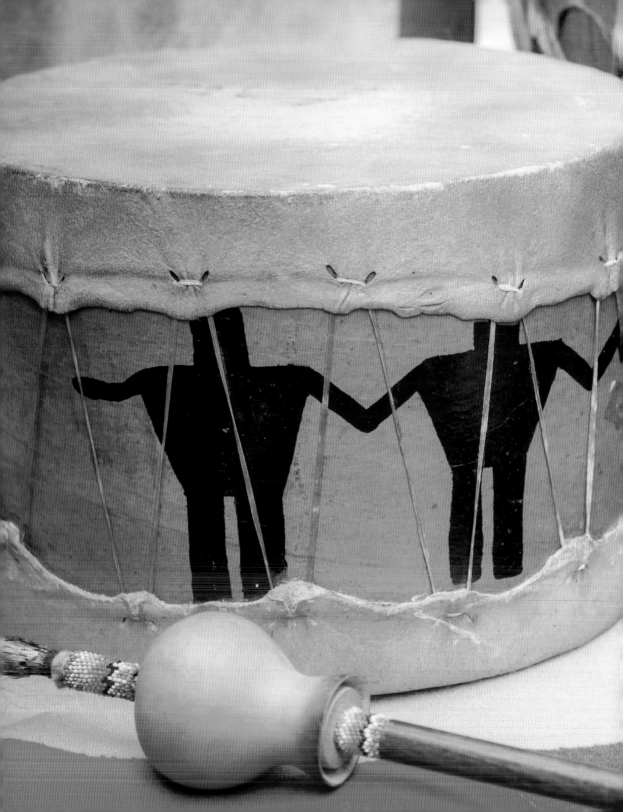

PART ELEVEN

TRANSFORMATION AND DRUMMING

No matter what they ever do to us, we must always act for the love of our people and the Earth. We must not react out of hatred against those who have no sense.

—JOHN TRUDELL (HUMAN BEING - DAKOTA)

Dealing with anger, again! Is fear related to anger? Is love related to anger? Do fear and love evoke anger? So many questions about anger . . . Who is not angry?

Sometimes I still wonder, when I see a turtle's body on the shore decapitated by a speedboat, or a river covered in toxic green algae, or the photo of someone, posing as a man, holding the head of an animal he has just shot for his own amusement. *What's not there to be angry about?*

However, I cannot imagine beating my anger on a drum. Those times I have been angry and needed to find peace of mind, I turned to the drum. Finding the song, or simply the rhythm I need to create peace of mind, is the goal of my drumming. *Remember,* I tell myself, *it's about raising the level of resonance . . .*

But I have never struck the drum in anger. Whether it's the hand drum, or the warrior's drum, they always have my gratitude and respect, and my love. Even on a warrior's drum, I have sung songs of destruction for those who wantonly defile this Earth, just as battle songs of the past evoked strength and courage to fight, and, if necessary, to kill. These were not songs of anger, though. I was taught that a warrior did not go into battle angry. So the idea of beating a drum in anger doesn't accord with my understanding of the drum. But, I would be the first to admit, my life's journey includes stages of anger into rage. When I was a young man, the drum gave me "A Chant to Lure Honor" as a way to deal with a phase of my life when anger could have ruined me as a teacher, just starting out on this journey. And there have been times, since then, when I felt the burn inside me and tasted the bitterness of anger. Again, the wisdom of those who keep the drum guided me to people and places that saved my life, to healers and ceremonies that would keep anger from destroying me.

CHAPTER THIRTY-SEVEN

THE DRUM JOURNEY INTO THE EARTH
AND OUT TO THE STARS

I never saw myself traveling to Washington, DC. Just the idea of Washington, DC, angered me, for this is the capital of the nation that tried to destroy what Indigenous people held sacred, what I hold sacred. It was the mid-nineties, and I had been invited to the nation's capital for a spiritual conference as a guest speaker, along with other folks, most notably, the holy man from the Amazon.

He was the reason I would go. He was the reason I was there.

So many things in life seem synchronous. I know Western science is catching on to this kind of thing, but researchers have to make a science out of it first. And that they have done. On the other hand, a Cherokee elder once told me this enticing idea in a simpler way: "It's just what happens when you're living in the Wheel."

Thinking I would pass some time and find a place to eat, I had just stepped out of the hotel elevator and into a sea of humanity filling the lobby. No one had to tell me. I could hear the whisperings. The crowd was awaiting the arrival of the "shaman from Brazil." When the elevator closed, I found myself unexpectedly against the lobby wall on the outer fringes of that ever-pressing sea.

In what appeared to be the next moment, what I first saw were the bright feathers of his headdress as he stepped through the glass turnstile doors into the midst of all the people. I watched the tips of the colorful feathers moving through the crowd, pausing and shaking as he was speaking to them, clasping hands, and quickly moving on, as though catching an ebb of current and riding it. And I'm sure I stood there in that subdued, angry state of mind, thinking how those in the crowd are all always about themselves: their needs, their time, their space. I was annoyed at them again, now because they had come between us, and even envious because their aggressive behavior got them to have a moment with him, while I could not.

Still, I remained transfixed as I watched the feathery tips of the headdress flow and bob through the sea of people until I noticed these beautiful feathers veer unexpectedly, as if a wave had suddenly crested and curled and broke, and the current was suddenly carrying him in my direction, and that is when I saw him.

I loved him. Immediately. Instantaneously. I don't know how, but I did. I loved him as a son loves a father he has missed throughout his life and with whom he has now been reunited. Whether he would see me or not, it didn't matter. Nothing could prevent this emergence of a son's love for his father. What this love can feel like. Just for that moment. He walked right up to me, smiled, and put his arms around me, embracing me and saying in my ear, "I came here because of you, Gabriel. I am your father."

I had learned early in life that you can't understand everything. You can try, and in trying to understand, you can help strengthen the spirit inside you. You can cause it to grow, but sometimes there does come a point when you just have to let things be. Accept what is. Accept what has happened. Maybe there is a logical or metaphorical explanation. Maybe there isn't. Maybe it just is what it is, and some things you simply can't explain; they just are what they are. *Of the Mystery.*

What I remember after that—between the moment of ceremony when the shaman's drum sent me farther away than even NASA could imagine, and then brought me back— is what I observed touring Washington, DC, the next day. I almost lost myself, for, in my mind, I had smashed glass windows, broken ropes, shoved people away. Scolded them. Shouted! *I hate what you've done to everything!* Yes, that was me; that was my anger consuming me. Perhaps you, too, have felt this kind of rage at some point in your life. Wanting to destroy what has hurt you. What has hurt the things and people you love. I had lost sight of any good.

What fueled my anger, when living became more than just about me, was the horror civilized humans, in particular, have inflicted on this world, and on this country they call

America. And I was feeling the anger I had already brought with me from my own life experiences. Anger began to devour me from the inside out.

Until the drum and song of the shaman took me away, very very far away, and then brought me back.

THE DRUMBEAT: PAY ATTENTION TO THE BEAT

We sat together, a few people, people I did not know, had not seen during the days of the spiritual conference, strangers who appeared as vague images, on the floor that evening after my "presentation," somewhere in the hotel in a dimly lit room. The holy man from deep in the Amazon, his tribe on the brink of extermination, held a small hand drum and a drumstick, and me, among people I didn't know, sitting in the circle with him. The anger and hurt I had experienced earlier that day, and the anger and frustration that had accumulated over various stages of my life, now occupied my physical form that was on the floor, crouched into a sphere, gripping my knees.

His instructions were to take only a single sip from the bowl that his wife, his companion, would offer. For a moment, the words he spoke did not seem to be English at all. But he must have been speaking in a way that I could comprehend because I understood everything he said. His wife, as conscientious as anyone can be arranging a sacred gift, prepared the small wooden bowl with the sacred drink. While she did, the holy man's drumming on the hand drum began, not much louder than my heart, it seemed, but each beat of his stick distinct. And then he began singing in a way I could only feel as a sacred song. And then, as if no time had passed at all, his wife bent toward me and gestured with the bowl. I took the sacred offering and sipped once. I had assumed it would taste harsh or unpleasant, but it was the sweetest taste I had, and have, ever experienced. Maybe because I was filled with so much bitterness.

It was easy to want more than the sip, the medicine tasted that good, but that was not how it should be. The shaman from the Star Nation people explained that he was going to begin the journey with a certain beat of the drum . . . "Like this . . . ," he said, demonstrating the sound, ". . . and then," he continued, "the beat will change . . . And this time, when you hear this beat," and again he expressed the sound with his drumstick on the drum, "you need to come back. Do not hesitate," he warned. "When you hear the changing of the drum's beat, come back."

As the drumming began, it wasn't long before I found myself running through a dense forest and soon realized that I was not a human running at all. I was a deer! I could feel my antlers. I could see them, like tree limbs, and I was flying past and under the branches of the trees. I could feel the power of the muscles in my legs and in my body. Everything about me was deer. My running took me down into the Earth. Such love, I exuded. Such beauty, I saw! Such power, I felt! When suddenly I began my ascent, and I was no longer a deer now, but had morphed into a dolphin swimming through Mother Ocean, and all the while, in my subconscious, I could hear the drumming . . . I was gliding. I was swimming. I was a dolphin.

I never stopped hearing the drumming.

This is what it is to be a dolphin, I was thinking. How wondrous! How alive! How joyful! How spirited! I am a dolphin! And then I was swimming straight up with such force that I broke the surface of the water and upward I continued, upward, and upward to the beat of the drumming I was a spirit speeding through the Sky, past the clouds, and then into space, and I was moving past the Moon, and my love for her filled me up, and I could see behind her the Earth, our Mother, and the Moon circling our Mother, and soon I saw the Sun, and the Earth circling the Sun, and farther out I was moving and I could see the solar system and farther and farther out I was at such a distance I could see the galaxy, the Milky Way, and I was drifting now, at the periphery of our galaxy, slowing at the point where I could barely make out where the sun was among the countless stars, and I felt the choice to keep going, and instinctively somehow knew that if I did, I would never come back, but why return? This was so beautiful.

And then I heard the drumbeat changing, and I didn't hesitate, and there in an instant I found myself still crouched on the floor, listening to the drumming and the sing-ing of this holy man next to me, and I could hear him weeping as he sang, and I could feel myself weeping with him, and now I was growing lighter, yet wondering, What is making him cry? Then he stopped, collapsed into exhaustion.

Ancient and contemporary stories abound of humans and animals shape-shifting. Every-where there are tribal peoples, stories are told about star beings from other worlds visiting Earth, and human beings from this world venturing out. Evidence of ancient celestial knowl-edge, and geological wisdom, often expressed through art and oral traditions, affirms this.

I got to feel the power of a deer, an animal with greater strength than any man could imagine. I got to feel his confidence, and his power, a life not intended to be a trophy hunter's murder victim. For that moment, while the shaman's drumbeat echoed in my brain, I was a force in nature, millions of years in the making. And I was a dolphin, know-ing the sacredness and embrace of our ocean, experiencing power and intelligence as no human could know—the life of our ocean.

And I traveled the stars!

And I got to see the Moon up close. And I got to experience what we look like from somewhere in our distant galaxy. I got to see the solar system, and the planets and incred-ible stars and travel through space and time, and I never needed a rocket of combustible toxic fuel to put me through a hole in our Sky.

A holy man, his drum, a sacred liquid, the drum, the holy man's instructions, the drum, the purpose of ceremony. So why was he crying?

Late that evening, I asked him. "Father, why were you crying?"

He leaned into me, held me with both hands, and put his lips close to my ear. "I was feeling what you were feeling, Gabriel," he said to me. "I was feeling your love, but I was crying because I was feeling your anger."

Indeed, the things that happen in the course of our journey influence us, and sometimes that influence can be detrimental to ourselves and to those around us. Yes, my anger could have consumed me. But now, I knew, it was time for me to pick up the drum and sing the old songs of healing and the new ones that would soon come.

I broke down and wept when I came home from that trip to Washington, DC, and from my journey into the Earth and into space. In my sorrow, loss, frustration, and even anger that had spent me, I crouched at the bottom of the pit of despair, and reached for the hand drum, and I beat my rhythm as it manifested, chanting a tribal song that emerged from a place somewhere near the heart of the Earth. A tribal song I would use to this day when despair and hopelessness threaten my happiness, and most importantly, when they threaten my gratitude.

And so, with drum in hand, the beat begins and the words are sent into the Mystery . . .

I feel like a leaf at the end of a branch of a thirsty tree.
I need something to sustain me.

And then switching my voice to the highest pitch I can I cry out in chanting . . .

Way hey yah / Way yah/
Way hey yah, way yah/
Way hey hey, way hey yah/
Way heehee yah / Way heeheehee yah

CHAPTER THIRTY-EIGHT

A WATER DRUM CEREMONY

Denny Cook Holmes

How do I begin to tell this story?

My first year to year and a half with the drum was spent in water drum ceremony with a Muscogee Creek medicine carrier sent by his church to travel and share this ceremony. So we gather in a circle of many, the circle having no beginning and no end. Gathering in a circle, there is a spirit of oneness that represents unity, integrity, and harmony. It is never ending.

The medicine man begins to tell us about the water drum, its meaning, and how it serves. The drum is made of wood and skin, filled with water and air, wrapped in a certain way with stones of a certain number and type, securing each location where the skin is tied over the mouth of the drum. He notes that the water within is poured back onto the Earth after the ceremony. Every step a ritual. The drum is the heartbeat of Earth and we sit in tempo with it, our unity and oneness centering around it. We are the circle and the heartbeat.

All become quiet as we begin, the rattle, the drumbeat, the song, the silence—the journey begins. The room is filled with a presence and a warmth, as if nothing else existed, as if embraced within the womb, safe and protected. During the ceremony at certain intervals we are asked to run our colors. This is done rapidly—red, orange, yellow, green, blue, indigo, violet—and then to see above our heads a white light filled with glowing amber flecks showering down over us like a waterfall.

At some point during the ceremony I find myself sitting in a field of green, sun shining down, lighting up all around me. I can feel the wind and feel the clear stream nearby. We are asked at this point to ask a question within of spirit. I do not know what to ask, so I put a simple question forward and ask to be told about my heart. There are no words spoken to me, but I look down in my lap and find my arms holding a doe. I remember the feeling of this embrace. The tenderness and gentleness of this innocent and most beautiful creature that had come to me. I still feel it to this day and just as I felt so warm, safe, and protected at the start of this ceremony I feel the same about the energy of this doe that I found within my own being. As if she is a part of my being now, held in my heart, I shield her and protect her essence within myself and in so doing am enabled to share that essence with others. I was shown my path. A path with heart and the grace and beauty of a doe. A constant reminder and awareness to me along this trail. Beautiful blessing and gift to be held sacred within my awareness always.

It is my understanding that the pouring of water from the drum afterwards onto the Earth represents forgiveness, as the water drum is a healing ceremony. Yet, for myself, forgiveness also encompasses gratitude. It is all a part of the circle.

—DENNY COOK HOLMES, A PRACTITIONER OF MEDITATION AND INDIGENOUS WAYS FOR OVER FORTY YEARS. SHE WRITES, "IT IS MY BELIEF THAT WE EXIST HERE AS SOULS IN HUMAN FORM SO ALL THAT WE ENCOUNTER IS TO PROPEL US FORWARD IN OUR WISDOM AND GROWTH AS SOULS."

PART TWELVE

LOVE AND LOSS AND HEALING

The Drums will always beat loudly in our hearts even through the noise of
the world, and every time your feet touch our Mother Earth, our souls will
feel the pull of those who walked before us.

—WILLIAM WINDWALKER

Music is the beat of a drum that keeps time with our emotions.

—SHANNON L. ALDER

CHAPTER THIRTY-NINE
THE DRUM AND THE SONGS

Looking back at the songs of the past, loss is part of the human condition, and the human condition proceeds from the Great Holy Mystery. This notion enables us to embrace such a gentle realization without sacrificing artistic and verbal embellishment, for we understand that our drums and the songs of our deepest and most bittersweet losses can be conveyed without oversentimentality. With the beat of our drums, we put the words into the Mystery. Some of those songs have been preserved and versions of them exist today. The idea remains to keep it simple, for we can get lost in our words, and certainly, the fewer we use, or need, the more profound and effective will be their power as they travel with the beating of heart and drum.

THE LOVER WHO DID NOT COME (AN OJIBWAY SONG)

A loon I thought it was,

But it was

My love's

Splashing oar . . .

My love

Has gone on before me.

Never again

Can I see him.

I imagine that no matter where they evolved on the Earth, human beings experienced loss, and so existed the need to express such loss with their most poetic and artistic renderings of heartache. Loss, as I understood the teachings, was not something overromanticized and overly sentimental. As we have heard these words in many forms, and as one of our great poet/philosophers, John Trudell, once sang, *It is what it is . . .*

Another realization exists when it comes to love: Not only can we have *our* hearts broken by another, but we can cause another's heart to break because of our actions as well.

Hold your drum, the drum you care for, the one who beats the rhythm of your pain and loss. The one who sustains the progression of your incantation reaching out to that *gentle realization* . . . And the beat begins . . . And we say/sing the words of the ancients . . . And the sounds we cry without words between the lines express the emotional meaning of how we feel . . . *Way Hey Yah! Way Hey Yah! Way Hey Yah Hey* . . . I once heard a hobbyist drum group performing for a university class. The young man who was the speaker for the group had stated that these sounds we make between the words, and the ones that accompany our emotions and the beat of the drum, were called "nonsensical." That was the word he used.

My uncles once wrote that "the soul of the poet/singer resides within the lines of his or her song, addressing the concept of the Great Mystery in them. Shared with the human being, the words and the beat ascend to the Great Mystery and, with their magic, bridge the distances that seem to exist between Earth and her mantle of enveloping air and the stars . . ." The drumming and the song evoke an owning-up affirmation to what we have done, and like a country that owns up to its own history, we begin the healing.

What Have I Done!
What have I done
That it feels I have torn the world apart?
And the Wind wails,
You have broken a heart.

Now your lover has gone and left you, but your longing continues . . .
Whenever I Think of Him . . .
Although he said it
Still
I am filled with longing
Whenever I think of him.

As your own heart aches, beat on your drum, the drum that you care for, the drum that you keep. Sing this song in the language you feel most comfortable using, for the Great Mystery does not translate. Sing the song, even if it means at first you talk the words; they will still become song, and know, that long ago, centuries, a thousand years and more, aching before you were ever born, there was another human heart who suffered such pain of loss . . .

LOVE SONG

No matter how hard I try
To forget you,
You always,
Come back to my mind,
And when you hear me singing
You may know I am weeping . . .

And on dying . . .

Nothing lasts long
But the Earth and the Sun
Way-hey hey-yah, way hey hey-yah

Nothing lasts long
But the Moon and the Stars
Way-hey hey-yah, way-hey hey-yah

HEALING WITH THE DRUM

Imagine holding a hand drum and singing similar words as they appear in an English translation from the Navaho's (Diné) "Beauty Way," from "The Night Chant," when the human condition is in need of restoration and help from the supernatural. Is this wrong? Is this appropriating a people's culture? Or is this a fusion, an adaptation and translation out of pure respect for what we need that we have lost and what they have shared? Is it something you committed to memory? The intent so strong you committed the words to memory, so that there is no mistake in the incantation? At times, because I don't use the songs often, I have them printed out in front of me so I can see them if I need to in order to sing them without error. Even for my own song, "A Chant to Lure Honor," because I don't sing it very often now, I use the printed words if I need them in front of me in order to *not* make an error. Of course, in this song of restoration, what the Diné singer is addressing is Diné understandings. Imagine, though, that these are human understandings as well . . . a being who shares the human condition and that condition springs forth from the Great Mystery.

Your offering I make.
I have prepared a smoke [tobacco] for you . . .

At this point, if I am using a drum to accompany the song to strengthen my depleted sense of self, I would address the spirit of the place around me, even if I have to travel in my mind to somewhere I know it is beautiful. Or, if I am in such a place physically, I express my intentions to the spirit of the place I am in, and I would use a pinch of tobacco in the pipe as an offering with the smoke, or if I do not have a pipe, to lay an offering of the leaves on the ground. I would want to be in a sacred space I have created for this occasion, even if it is a niche I have helped create in the city. Even if it is in a prison. No matter where I am, the choices I made somehow lead me to this place, and though it may not be conducive to ceremony, I know the song will transform my mind, and I will begin to drum, or if I don't have access to a drum, I imagine one, and I use what I can to create a beat—a rapid, steady, soft, and even quiet beat—for I am a human being in need of restoration . . .

House made of dawn,
House made of evening light,
House made of cloud,
House made of rain,
House made of dark mist,
House made of female rain,
House made of pollen,
House made of grasshoppers,
Dark cloud is at the door,
The trail out of it is dark cloud,
The zigzag lightning stands high upon it . . .

Your offering I make.

I have prepared a smoke for you.

Restore my feet for me.

Restore my legs for me.

Restore my body for me.

Restore my mind for me.

Restore my voice for me.

This very day take out your spell for me.

Your spell remove for me.

You have taken it away from me;

Far off it has gone.

Happily I recover.

Happily my interior becomes cool.

Happily I go forth.

My interior feeling cool, may I walk.

No longer sore, may I walk.

Impervious to pain, may I walk.

With lively feelings, may I walk.

As it used to be long ago, may I walk.

Happily may I walk.

Happily with abundant dark clouds, may I walk

Happily with abundant showers, may I walk.

Happily with abundant plants, may I walk.

Happily, on the trail of pollen, may I walk.

Happily may I walk.

Beings as it used to be long ago, may I walk.

May it be beautiful before me.

May it be beautiful behind me.
May it be beautiful below me.
May it be beautiful above me.
May it be beautiful all around me.
In beauty it is done.

CHAPTER FORTY

HEALING DEER DRUM

Jeannine Wiest

To listen to the drum is also to feel oneself listened to by the drum.

I know that now. I had forgotten.

Three years ago, when I began trembling, I didn't resonate at all with drums. Oh, I did like the moment in the Beach Boys song, "Wouldn't It Be Nice," when there's a pause in the refrain followed by a short, swift kick-drum sound. Satisfying as that moment is, alas, for many years it was my only positive drum recollection.

But I never imagined there was different drumming to embrace. Never dreamt it could take hold of my internal alarm system and envelope it completely, swaddle my system so that my nerves and brain might sort themselves out.

Yet, now, I can find sonic solace anywhere in nature. Even the midnight rain drumming on the roof coaxes the beating of my heart into sensory reciprocity.

When I began exhibiting symptoms of what would eventually be diagnosed as essential tremor, some friends fell away, some merely looked away, and one friend gave me a deer-hide drum. It was made by the Lummi tribe, the Lhaq'temish, from Washington State, known as the people of the sea.

Since I was now unable to keep a reliable beat, I thought the gift odd, but said thanks as I mentally planned in which closet to hide the offending reminder of my disorder.

Then I was inundated with armchair advice.

"Just shake," my friend Graywolf said. Sage advice. However, I wasn't at the stage to allow and embrace it just yet.

"It's an ancestral manifestation. Release it," said a healer friend. Maybe, but I nearly hauled off and smacked that pat solution from her lips.

"Isn't there something the doctors can do?" a conservative pal asked. It turns out there isn't much.

That wasn't entirely a bad turn of events because, otherwise, I wouldn't have met my sonic match in a deer drum.

I'm not saying I was Zen about trembling. Actually, I panicked. I've always made my living with my hands: first, dancer hands, then costume designer hands, then writer hands, then, ultimately, healer hands.

Believing that I was no longer the steadiest pendulum in the room, nor the most grounded presence, I vowed to find a way to work around this nonessential tremor (as I began referring to the trembles).

I renewed my creative noticing practice that I teach other women. I actively courted sympathetic resonance, the principle of music, which explains the magic of vibrational attraction.

I felt pulled to travel to a sacred space on a hill in Ojai, California. The leader of the space had a drum similar to my gift drum, but much wider in circumference—embellished—befitting a drumming elder.

There, I experienced a healing of my luminous energetic body via a Peruvian shamanic drumming meditation. The powerful drumming put me into parasympathetic mode, so that my body had the opportunity to begin its healing process. I was still for the first time in a long while.

In music, sympathetic resonance explains the reason that, if you walk into a room full of pianos and play a middle C on one, all the other unplayed pianos in the room start vibrating to the frequency of middle C.

I had forgotten, in my panic over the diagnosis, that when exploring sonic healing, we access the internal harmonic beat that develops when the natural vibration frequency of one mechanism is in phase with a vibration of another mechanism. The connection from piano resonance to vibrationally humming humans is visceral.

Drum resonance, however, is primal, earthy and the healing feels like a mirroring dance.

Do I still shake? Yes. But I have a connection to the sonic field that has been waiting to catch my ear. My deer drum had been waiting to begin a pulsing conversation with me for a long time. How long? My drum whispers, "Forever."

—JEANNINE WIEST, AUTHOR OF *THE ALCHEMY OF SELF-HEALING* AND CREATOR OF THE INNER WISDOM RECOVERY CLASSES.

A HEALING SONG

The Earth and Sky need time to heal.
Animals need time to heal.
Birds and insects need time to heal.
And plants and trees,
And lakes and ponds
And rivers and oceans, each needs time to heal.
Dolphins need time to heal,
And whales,
And shellfish and fish,
All need time to heal.
Men need time to heal.
Women need time to heal.
And our children need time to heal.

Now, in the healing time,
Now, in the healing time.

PART THIRTEEN

THANKSGIVING AND PASSING ON TRADITION

With one mind we address our acknowledgement, respect, and gratefulness to all the sacred Cycle of Life. We, as humans, must remember to be humble and acknowledge the gifts we use so freely in our daily lives.

—AUDREY SHENANDOAH (ONONDAGA) FROM *WISDOMKEEPERS*

Whenever a ceremony begins, when the hearts of the people join in solemn and sacred prayer, or a council convenes to deliberate and decide on issues of the People, all those who assemble begin by expressing gratitude to all that has sustained them.

—FROM *THE BOOK OF CEREMONIES*

CHAPTER FORTY-ONE

THANKSGIVING AS A HISTORY AND A CULTURE

Princess Red Wing was my godmother, and she had taught me, as well as almost every person who gave her the opportunity, that there was not just one Thanksgiving for the Indigenous people long ago. "There was a Thanksgiving for each full moon," she said. Thirteen squares on a turtle's back, thirteen full moons in a year. I had also learned from other elders when I was younger that this was, indeed, the time to express gratitude, and to also ask Grandmother Moon during her time of fullness, to take away anything that might be causing me pain, ask her if she would lift away any obstacles that were preventing me from walking the path of heart and fulfilling my purpose. But, always be advised, they said, that you choose your words carefully, Gabriel. Think about what you are saying before you say it. Words have power . . . Words have consequence.

They say that long ago, great drums were made from turtle shells, but they were rare, as turtles were so revered and such a shell should not be taken without sacrifice and vision. It has been said that the heart of a turtle often beats long after the turtle has died. Not long ago, on the sands of the Gulf of Mexico, Amy and I discovered a turtle's body on the beach. It was a most gruesome reminder that no one has a stronger heart than a turtle. I described to Amy, whose blindness was sparing her the visual horror, that the turtle's face was almost gone. My daughter, whose environmental work involves protecting our waters, had also walked up to the gruesome scene. She had deduced that the propeller of a speeding Jet Ski®, or even a racing speedboat, had hit the great turtle.

Still, we could see her trail in the sand heading up to the base of the dunes. Beyond severely injured, she had managed to make it to shore, ascend the beach, dig her nest, and lay her eggs. We could also see the trail back. With her two-hundred-million-year purpose fulfilled, she died a short distance from the ebbing tide as she struggled without a face to return to her own Mother, the Ocean.

Again, the power of a turtle's heart has no measure, and such a shell must never be taken casually, or greedily, but with absolute grief and respect and spiritual acknowledgment. Even painting a turtle on a drum, or a rattle, requires awareness of the symbolism.

I had been taught about the various kinds of Thanksgivings. And yes, there were more than one. There were four major Thanksgivings, Red Wing had explained, and a fifth as well. This is the one that took place as a result of what is now called Indian summer. It's that time in late fall when the warm breezes from the South come North and allow those beings—whether they be human, animal, or bird, who are not quite as fast and industrious as others—to gather their food sources in as well. It is a time of Thanksgiving for the cranberries, too. They are the fruit that may taste a little bitter because, as Red Wing said, the sweetness of creation had been used up in the other berries. Then the Maple Syrup Thanksgiving occurs as we approach spring. Did you know the first ice-cream cone a colonist ever saw was being enjoyed by Indian children as they licked the ice from the cones their grandmothers and mothers made, dipping the ice on the top of the cone in maple syrup?

Then there is the Strawberry Moon Thanksgiving as the solstice of summer nears. "And remember," Red Wing said, "we never quarrel in the presence of strawberries. No one should listen to the drum at the strawberry festival, or dance, carrying a grudge."

Of course, in the middle of summer there is the Green Bean Thanksgiving, reminding us of the power in even the littlest things of Earth, which provide sustenance that we may live. And the Thanksgiving that all Americans are aware of is the Harvest Thanksgiving.

As I imagine in the days before the arrival of the first Europeans to this land, during these Thanksgiving occasions, especially, Native songs on the drums were sung and danced. The drums were always present and beating during these times of expressed appreciation.

Even as I recall these teachings, I can still see in my memory and imagination Princess Red Wing holding her hand drum in one hand and her stick in the other, beating the drum as she delivered the message, the drum that beat with the heart of Earth, the heart of people, and the heart of the universe. Of course, Red Wing went on to share more of the story of the colonists' first Thanksgiving, and who else to tell this story than the direct descendant of those who greeted the pilgrims? No doubt, other versions exist, even among the Native people whose ancestors were there, but one fact is obvious among each: that without the help of the Indian, the first immigrants to what is now commonly known as New England would have perished.

"The pilgrim colony had lost their harvest," she said with the certainty of ancestral blood that only generations of storytelling could affirm. As when they first stepped upon these beautiful shores, the early Europeans were in dire straits, and the Wampanoag mothers opened their storehouses of food and helped them survive, gave them seeds for planting, and showed them how . . . And still, they could not make a go of it alone. Many died. She said that when Squanto overheard the complaints of Governor William Bradford in his prayers of frustration to God, and the sad and desperate cries of the first pilgrims for wont of sustenance, Squanto took pity on them. And so, he counseled with his Wampanoag people and with their Massasoit, Osamekum.

"'Brother,' he said to Bradford, 'now is not the time to mourn your terrible loss of friends and family, your lack of food that makes you hungry. Show that you are grateful, even now, and express gratitude for what you have . . .'" And with that, Squanto invited the pilgrims to share in that bountiful Indigenous Harvest Thanksgiving, which became the colonists' first Thanksgiving. That's how Red Wing told the story.

But, as we know, the story didn't end there. My uncles Nippawanock and Metacomet added that the pilgrims would only allow themselves to be served by the Indians on that Thanksgiving Day. And, they did not allow the Indians to sit with them at the same table. Now I think to myself how many schoolchildren dress up as Indians and pilgrims during Thanksgiving, and the teachers have them each serving food and sharing the same table, and I thought of this as just one more example of how, as America has taught its history, the Indians have been essentially left out, except where they are convenient, like at Thanksgiving (though they seem to be removing them from that occasion as well—slowly but surely, we see more pilgrims, bigger parades). Or consider the romanticized versions of Pocahontas, or Sacagawea. Or the stereotyped mascot or name for a sports team. It has been said that if we do not know where we came from, how will we know where we are going? And how sad for children who aren't taught that history . . . How sad for America, and how devastating for the Earth.

CHAPTER FORTY-TWO

THE WARRIOR'S DRUM RESONATES ON THANKSGIVING

It's Thanksgiving. Not much different from last year. Our family sits in a circle on couches and chairs and pillows on the floor. A feast of Indigenous foods awaits in the kitchen. But something is different today. Very different. More different than it ever has been on Thanksgiving Day at our house. My daughter Calusa has a baby growing in her womb she has already named Alsea. My grandchild has been given a name in the same spirit Calusa received hers; Alsea will carry with the sound of her name the memory of an extinct Indigenous people who once thrived in America. Their memory will live on in the sound of her name.

"Children," I say, though Calusa and her two brothers, Ihasha and Carises, are each in their thirties and married now with partners sitting with them, "I need to ask you something. I would like to present the Thanksgiving Address today, but this time, I will need a drum."

I looked at my beautiful daughter, her belly swollen with life. Her hands on her belly. She is warm and somewhat uncomfortable in her own body. I can tell. For I have known her since before she was born. Behind me on the bookshelf stands a photograph of me holding Calusa in my arms as an infant. I touched her with an eagle feather as soon as she was born. The feather remained with her during infancy. "I feel we need to do this address with the drum," I continued, "because it is Alsea's first Thanksgiving."

"I have two drums," I said. "One is the hand drum I have used many times." I paused, smiling at the human beings gathered in the small living room. "But I have made the warrior's drum available as well."

I looked at my daughter. I had discussed this with Amy earlier. Amy is wise, and she is loving. And, as always, I needed her insight. She knows Calusa is a warrior and that I had asked a respectful question. I remember my uncles telling me that grandparents often walked a precarious line when it comes to their children's children. *Try and always respect the boundaries*, they said. *It's tough sometimes*, they added. *Nonetheless, there are boundaries, and it can be risky.*

"Calusa," I said, gazing at her. She never looked more beautiful, even as she scooched around the chair trying to find a comfortable position for the daughter inside her. "It will be your decision which drum we should use today. Which drum will be the first Alsea will hear? Now they are both powerful drums, though the hand drum may be softer and not frighten her. The warrior's drum, well, I think you know the power of such a sound. Like thunder! I would be so honored to sing this sacred address, using one of these drums, so this would be Alsea's first."

True to her own warrior nature, even as she prepares to give life to the world, Calusa didn't hesitate. "I think you know which one, Dad," she said, and smiled. I looked at her, not saying, not volunteering, the words that could only come from her. "The warrior's drum."

CHAPTER FORTY-THREE

A THANKSGIVING ADDRESS

The thunder of the warrior's drum boomed! Once. Twice. Again. And again. Four times as Red Wing had always done before she gave an address. One for each direction, she would say.

And that evening when it was my turn to speak and sing the words that I first had heard Red Wing utter, then her sons, my uncles, we sat—their family, our family, one family—in that circle with no beginning and without end. Each was ever mindful of this new life, Alsea, within the circle of life that we had formed there in the living room of our small home on Thanksgiving.

The drumming was powerful as the drumming is on the warrior's drum. Out of the corner of my eye I caught a glimpse of Calusa holding her belly. Her hands wrapped around her daughter, in what appeared as a loving embrace.

"Thank you, oceans and bays!" I began. *The beating of the drum powerful and steady* . . . "Rivers and streams and little brooks and creeks . . ." *Steady beating* . . . "Quiet Pools and Lakes, thank you . . .

"Fish, and shellfish . . . " *steady beat* . . . "big and small who have given of yourselves that we may live . . . THANK YOU!" *Boom! Boom! And the drumming continues as the spoken words become the song* . . .

"Whales . . . our cetacean relatives . . . Thank You . . . for your wisdom . . . ! And the lessons of family you have taught us . . . for all you have given us . . . and to your cousins . . . oh dolphins! . . . For the joy you have brought us, and the sense of elation you give us, and love you have shown us. Thank you!

"Corn Maiden and Wild Rice . . . ! Foods rooted in the land! Fruits and berries, medicinal plants and trees, forests and standing nations, Thank You for the shelter you provide and the air we breathe . . .

"Thank you, animals, great and small, who have served for food, giving unselfishly of yourselves that we may live, and who have shared with us your power and your wisdom." *The drumming has become the song . . .*

"Thank you, beautiful winged-beings, from the hummingbird to the osprey, from the sparrow to the eagle. Your feathers have adorned us and serve as the intercessors of our prayers. Our world would be empty without you, THANK YOU!

"Tiny insects who help keep the balance. Thank you.

"Father Sky, who protects us and our Mother, the Earth, THANK YOU.

"Mother Earth, THANK YOU for sustaining us. Thank you for loving us!

"Elder relative, oh Mighty Sun, for your gift of life and light and warmth, THANK YOU!

"Sacred Moon, precious and powerful and mysterious. THANK YOU for influencing the movements of the waters, and the cycles of women and men and harvest. THANK YOU for helping to keep the Earth revolving! We love you.

"To the winds of the four directions. To the great winds that sweep away the illusions of our world and of our self-importance, and to the gentle breezes that caress our senses, Thank You.

"Thunder beings, THANK YOU for bringing the rain that sustains life, and the lightning that connects Sky and Earth!

"Relatives and messengers who dwell among the stars, Thank you.

"Source of All Things, who exists in all things and within all things, who always was and will forever be, Great Holy Mystery, THANK YOU!"

CHAPTER FORTY-FOUR

DRUM CIRCLES

No matter what their shape, a circular energy seems to emanate from traditional drums. Each beat I imagine as rings of vibrations going out into the world, into the Mystery, going deeper into self. A sort of quantum physics of an Indigenous kind.

Circles within circles, with no beginning and no ending. Oneness. Completeness. Continuation. And thus my life . . .

In my seventieth year of this remarkable journey, I glance back in memory at the people, events, and circumstances that were intimately connected to my path, and it blurs, twinkles, and blurs, like gazing up at the stars when your eyes are tearful.

I cried during the death songs sung on the drums to say good-bye to my students: the ones killed in car accidents, the ones murdered, and the ones who committed suicide. I've cried with the death songs on the beating drum for those beloved beings, human and nonhuman, who loved me.

But my tears have not fallen only out of grief, out of sorrow. I've cried for the blessings in my life as well. For thanksgiving springs from my heart for each day I am alive. Each day I feel my heartbeat in rhythm is a thanksgiving. Each day I can tell my wife and children and grandchildren, and Mother Earth, and the Sun, and the Sky, and the Moon, and the birds, and the animals, and the fish and shellfish, and the dolphins, and mantas and rays, and the plants and the flowers and the trees, and the ocean, the bees and the butterflies, that I love them and can beat on the drum this love . . . is a Thanksgiving.

Circles. Circles within circles. As nature intended, painful, challenging, demanding, magical, wonderful, joyful, and serendipitous.

When my children were born, they were named for extinct Indigenous tribes and nations. I have from time to time incanted their names on the drum in a special song just for their names. One idea for giving them such names was to keep the vibration of the tribal word as proof of their existence in the world. Through memory, they still can exist. Even the great minds of science have affirmed: Everything is vibration. Life is vibration. Another reason for giving my children these names was that each comes from "A Chant to Lure Honor." They are sung on the drum each time I sing the chant . . . The vibrations live on in their names.

Of course, the children of such names would carry the burden of that responsibility.

Circles within circles. With no beginning and no end . . .

My daughter and son-in-law chose for their daughter, my first granddaughter, a name from a tribe also driven to extinction, no longer dwelling as a tribal entity on the Earth. She is named Alsea. They were a tribe known, among many things, to have elongated heads that anthropologists believe was purposely done to mimic the beauty of the ancients, the ancestors that some of our people to this day call the star people.

Circles within circles . . .

I was holding Alsea a few weeks after her birth, and I asked my daughter Calusa for permission to use the drum that Princess Red Wing had passed on to her. I wanted to drum for my granddaughter. With my daughter's permission I lifted the drum from her special place on the shelf, and began drumming for my granddaughter, as softly as I could, and chanting her name in whispers.

Circles within circles. Oneness. Completeness. Continuation. No beginning. No ending. We live!

Amy and I had to leave our home for a few days while needed work was being done on the house. Thanks to good friends, we had a place to stay where we could bring our dog and cat along as well. But without any protection, we couldn't leave the pipe and the drums. Problem. The warrior's drum, the grandfather drum, had become too heavy for me to carry and place safely in the car.

I am older now than even my uncles were when they passed the great drum on to me. Not long after that, they made their Great Change. They died. Though I would like to remain here for as long as I can, the realization was simple when I realized I could not carry the drum to the car without risk—to the drum and to me. I needed to do as my elders had done, and it was time for me to ask my oldest son if he would take the responsibility of the warrior's drum. For the tradition I was taught is to ask the oldest son first. And I did.

Circles. No beginning. No ending. Fulfillment. Completeness. Continuation.

Now in my son's care, may the drum be loved and cared for, and may he resonate for the next generation!

INDEX

Note: Page numbers in parentheses indicate non-contiguous references.